REVIE

MW01226622

"So many women will recognise themselves in your words and so many people will become aware of the pain inside so many souls amongst us... Pain we cannot see from the outside so it takes guts to start conversations that leads to connections that leads to understanding, but above all that it takes love."

— Francis, from Holland

"A heroic, engaging, honest look into the life of a courageous woman. As Carla struggles to overcome the brutalizing effects of early sexual and emotional abuse, she shows us all the power of individual spirit. Her journey is ultimately a testimony to a strong, spiritual woman's belief in herself. Thank you, Carla, for a great read."

— Sharky, Life Artist from Mexico, originally from USA

"This story is a timely reminder to us all that we must shine a light into the shadows and expose those not so pretty parts of ourselves. The poetry interwoven amongst the pages is honest and raw. It reminds us that this process is necessary on the path to healing."

— A. R., from Canada

"You've painted an evocative description of your experiences and there is a nice overall arc throughout showing the development of your spirituality and how you've learned about yourself, your needs, and self-expression. It's a very encouraging story for others who are suffering or trying to recover themselves."

— Ken, Proofreader/Editor, USA

"The unexpected gift of motherhood, the travelling, the perseverance to stay in this world in spite of very painful times—how that all contributed to your open heart, to challenging those demons and replacing the belief that you were not worthy of love, of being cared for and respected just for being you. It is so incredible that you have become a woman who can trust intuition, listen to your boundaries, let go of the mask and be good with who you are. The poetry is so profound, and the summary is awesome."

— Child Therapist from Canada

"This gripping, heartfelt page turner will connect you forever with Carla."

— Susan from Mexico, originally from Canada

"Not only does it contain an uplifting message (you overcoming adversity in the past), it's also a very interesting read. It was great to read how well and quickly your career progressed in spite of receiving limited education and, the nudist cruise was a very brave and colorful experience to write about! Living in so many different countries also makes for interesting reading."

— K. from USA

"This hard-won path to self-love and compassion and self-acceptance is very inspiring, and I am glad you found your voice to write about it all."

— C.S. from Canada

"Overall the message is so powerful—of how, given all of the abuse and disrespect and lack of capacity for safe and unconditional love in your adults and family, the destructive beliefs were inevitably and understandably embedded and entrenched in your being, and how you have been working to challenge those beliefs and reach compassion and self-love and acceptance—what an incredibly powerful message that shone through in a very moving and inspiring way."

— C. from Canada

"This book has me thinking of my life experiences and how they've affected me. Perhaps the same will happen with other readers."

— Gilles, from Canada

"Chapter 4 was very difficult for me to read because it brought back a lot of memories that I needed to meditate on... That night, I did not get much sleep... Of course, as usual, I did what Matt Khan would say... Whatever arises, love that... I sure did a lot of loving that night...so thank you for helping me remember what needed to be awakened, acknowledged, honored, and loved. :)"

— Sophie, from Canada

"The book is very easy to understand and it is easy to relate to your stories! I truly enjoyed reading the poetry that was included in your book! They really spoke to me. 👍"

— S. D., from Canada

"I cannot wait to recommend this book to others as it will be a beacon of hope to some and an all too familiar story to many."

— Angela P., from Canada

A Life Worth Living

The Journey of an Authentic Soul

By

Carla Feagan

A Life Worth Living; The Journey of an Authentic Soul
By Carla Feagan

Copyright © 2018 by Carla Feagan, Divine Press

For more about this author please visit www.carlafeagan.com

This is a work of nonfiction. The events in this book are portrayed to the best of Carla Feagan's memory. While all the stories in this book are true, some names and identifying details have been changed to protect the privacy of the people involved.

All rights reserved. No part of this publication may be reproduced, distributed, or transmitted in any form or by any means, including photocopying, recording, or other electronic or mechanical methods, without the prior written permission of the publisher, except in the case of brief quotations embodied in critical reviews and certain other noncommercial uses permitted by copyright law.

For permission requests: press@carlafeagan.com
Divine Press
www.carlafeagan.com

Ordering Information: Quantity sales. Special discounts are available on quantity purchases by corporations, associations, and others. Orders by U.S. trade bookstores and wholesalers. For details, contact the publisher at the email address above.

Proofreading by The Pro Book Editor
Book Cover Design by Tugboat Design
Author Picture by Cat Eye Creations

ISBN: 978-1-7752609-1-2

1. BODY, MIND & SPIRIT / Inspiration & Personal Growth
2. BIOGRAPHY & AUTOBIOGRAPHY / Personal Memoirs

First Edition

Dedicated to my mother, whose power and strength helped her overcome what life had handed her. I now understand and forgive without hesitation. Also, to my children, Michael and Tandia: you taught me what it means to be a mother and to strive to become who I AM today.

Amidst the reawakening, she found that she was lost.
Unsure what to believe and unsure what to forget.
Her words were never wrong nor right,
but at that moment she felt the light.
The warmth it brought to her and the fright that left.
Her mind was set still and her body wary.
In this moment, the ground grew and the sky sank.
Everything she had thought began to dissipate.

By Tandia Mercedes Feagan

CONTENTS

PREFACE

"You are a healer." I hear these words come from someone I do not know. A stranger, standing there pensively and speaking to me.

My immediate thoughts are *What are you saying? No, I am not, and who are you to be telling me this? I am a logical person. I have been an accountant, a computer programmer, a businessperson, a salesperson, a manager. What do I know about healing?* This is not the first person to say this to me. I have heard this message repeatedly from many different people from many different backgrounds, from people who do not know each other, and people who do not know me or who I am. The message is always the same, "You are a healer." It makes me confused as they certainly do not know what they are talking about. It perplexes me as I am not a healer. I am hurt. I am a victim. I am a survivor. I am the one who needs to be healed, not the one doing the healing. How do I know how to heal anyone? Where is my area of expertise? What time have I spent learning a discipline on how to heal someone? Anyone. This was a very confusing part of my life.

The messages started back in 2009. As I look back I can literally feel the confusion. I also want to say anger. Anger is in the back of my mind, so I must write it down. Anger at having the message delivered in so many ways that I cannot ignore it. Anger at not knowing what it means. Anger for teasing me, accusing me of something that I am not. Anger at not being able to heal myself, let alone other people. Yes, anger is there lurking stealthily behind the confusion.

Who am I? Why am I here? Why have I gone through the experiences that I have? Why do I still want to end my life? Why is there still so much hurt and pain? What did I do so wrong? What is wrong with me? These are the questions that go around and around in my head, like a never-ending story. These beliefs and feelings were so ingrained into my being that I could not understand the message being delivered. This memoir will show where these negative beliefs originated and what I did to release them, to allow them to dissipate and no longer rule my life.

It is funny, not funny ha-ha but funny strange. As I was growing up and going through all my experiences, I had a strength inside of me that would not let me give up, not let me give in. I do not know how or why, but it was there, all the time, like a sneaky little idea, or thought, or knowing. It kept me alive. It kept me trying; it kept me going; it kept me wanting to love with openness. I kept running into walls. I kept picking myself up and doing it all over again. It was a strength that was bigger than me, deeper than me, submerged in me, helping me, holding me. I always kept the thought in the back of my mind, *I can do this.* Even through the suicide attempts, *I can do this.* So many attempts, so many failed tries as the world of pain engulfed me. As I was trying to hang myself when I was nine… as I write this I feel a tightening in my neck, my breath becomes shallow…I feel the noose getting tighter. It feels…good; it makes me feel the physical of what I have known emotionally. The cutting off of my voice. My inability to speak. Not being heard. The cries of my soul to help me as I see no hope. I ask myself, *Why does a nine-year-old girl feel no hope? How does one so young get to the point of wanting to kill herself?* The truth lies in the story. A story I have told countless times. A story I can now tell with few emotions. A story that was given to me in order to learn from it. For here I sit, at fifty-two years of age, still alive and now writing.

This is a story that will resonate with a lot of people, too many people. It is rather sad that so many people have been through or know someone who has gone through rough periods in their life. Rough enough to contemplate taking their own life. I am here because there was a stronger force behind me, a stronger force that kept me alive, not allowing me to go through with it, not to end it; but there was a need to see, to understand, how desperate someone can get in order to even consider it. I am you, and this is our story. A story filled with trials and tribulations, happiness and sadness, crying and laughing; a story to make one believe that they are worth it. There is a reason for them on this planet at this point in time. This is a story that I was told I needed to write by my beautiful soul sister, Sherry, during the first tarot card reading I had with her. This was at the same time that I was being told I was a healer. These are the messages that I have been ignoring. Well, that I tried to ignore. This story is about being vulnerable, opening the dark secrets that one tries to hide, taking off the mask and allowing the *me* of who I AM to emerge.

In all honesty, I have started, and stopped, the writing of this story many times. I have since come to acknowledge that it is the deep-seated root of not being worthy that was stopping me. I still have remnants of that root. However, it does not have the power over me that it once did. This is my story of hurt and healing, and the realizations that I have had along this journey of mine called life.

I have to say, one of the reasons why I had a hard time starting was that my truth would inadvertently hurt people in my life. Therefore, some names and places have been modified to protect those people. Have I forgiven? For the most part, yes. However, I have since realized that forgiveness is not the end. It is a stepping stone to understanding. The understanding of what that person was going through that would enable them to do horrific things to another. Be it right, or be it wrong, everyone has a story, a reason, a purpose for doing the things that they have done. Some will never fully understand the repercussions of what they did. Some will never even know that they did wrong. It is not up to me to explain to them or tell them or make them understand. Those are their lessons to learn. My lesson has been to take full control over how I felt, how I feel, and to move onward, so that I may gain greater clarity into the truth of who I AM.

To everyone who has had a part in my life, I thank you. I am blessed to have you in my existence, as I would not be who I am today if it were not for you.

There is a person, who I have to acknowledge, for being the catalyst for me starting to write. I met Brendan in June of 2017. He is a Scotsman from Amsterdam and was on vacation in Playa del Carmen, MX, where I live. Sometimes in life you meet someone who instantly resonates with you. It was like meeting a long-lost friend, someone you are immediately comfortable with. Soul mate, twin flame, it doesn't really matter what you call it. It is real, and it is amazing. We spent five wonderful days together before he left to go back home. In any case, we kept talking and chatting and texting constantly, almost obsessively, for the first few weeks after he left. He was making plans to move to Playa del Carmen for a few months to test it out. Well, as it happens in life, reality set in for him when he got back, as work was very busy. He had a lot of visitors from out of town and his plans kept changing. We still keep in contact, albeit not as much as those first few weeks, and I had a beautiful conversation with him on August 24, 2017, about how he still wanted to come to Mexico, but external, material things kept getting in the way. My heart went out to him as I felt his confusion. He was totally in his mind, leaving his heart behind. When I got up on the morning of August 25, the following three poems came out of nowhere. I mean nowhere as I am not a poet, I've never thought of writing poetry, and it surprised me as the words poured out from my soul to my hands to words on paper.

Let Go of the Mind

Let go of the mind
as the mind distracts
by supplying endless decisions
decisions that whirl around
into endless thinking
endless thinking turns into confusion
and confusion leaves one stuck
stuck in indecision.

Instead

Go into the heart
the heart knows your true path
the path that allows you to
jump
into the flow
of the universal river.
The flow that will guide you
and take you on a journey
that you know to be true.

Truth

Truth
lies in the perceptions of the beholder
the stories,
the beliefs,
the lessons,
the fears,
the knowing,
the unknowing
all makes up the ideology of truth.
What is true to one
is false to another
so who is to say what is universal truth?

No one knows
one can only go internally
to discover truth for themselves
to have wisdom
to know that one's own truth
is only true for them
in that moment and time
for even truth can become false
if circumstances change.

By listening to one's heart
at every second of every day
one can know truth in that moment.

By being open to change
destroying the box that one lives in
opening one's heart
and listening to its whispers

sets one free
to discover the truth that lies within.

A Life Truly Lived

A life truly lived
contains happiness and fear
resentment and loathing
bliss and fulfillment
contentment and unhappiness.

A life truly lived
goes through all the emotions
to define the lessons that one needs to learn
to move up and beyond the illusion of what is expected
to take off the mask
to become authentic
to allow the heart to open
and the mind to stop its incessant nagging.

A life truly lived
is to listen to the whispers of the soul
to hear and speak through the heart
to love unconditionally
to let go of expectations.

A life truly lived
is to be
here
now
in this presence.

The poem *Truth* keeps coming back to me as I write my truth about my life. I'm aware that others who are a part of this memoir will remember things differently. That is OK. It is what it is meant to be. Everyone remembers things differently and everyone who reads this will be affected differently.

This book, my memoir, has been written in order to bring light into the dark, to allow people to know that they are not the only ones that have gone through a tragic path. One can release the beliefs that were ingrained at an early age, to be able to live a life they truly deserve.

A Life Worth Living

The Journey of an Authentic Soul

CHAPTER 1

1961 to 1972

South Africa, Singapore and England

"Stand aside, the whites are coming," the tour guide yelled. Our tour group stepped off the walkway to let a group of white people pass. I was confused, this was the first time I had been referred to as non-white, my first and only experience of racism. It was in 1974 and I was nine years old when my family and I went on a vacation to South Africa. While we were there we visited the Congo Caves. This is when I hear these words. Apartheid in full force. I had no idea at the time what this was or what it meant. You see, my parents were both born in Cape Town, South Africa in 1938. Apartheid did not start until 1948. But apartheid had lumped everyone who was not completely white into a group called "colored's" or "blacks" and racism became rampant. Whites were superior. My parents are both of mixed heritage, German, Filipino, English, Polynesian, and a few more nationalities that I cannot remember. My mom was not what I consider colored as she was olive skin toned, and my dad, well, he was certainly darker. For some reason I don't like the word black. None the less, they were not white, they were colored. My parents never talked about their life in South Africa, or how apartheid affected them. I can only imagine what it must have been like at the age of ten to have your entire life disrupted because of your skin tone.

My grandfather on my dad's side had a mechanic shop and owned a property on a beach around Cape Town. During apartheid, it was deemed that colored's were not allowed to own anything of significant value. So the beach property was taken away from him and given to the whites. My father and his brothers, many, many years later, maybe in 2012 or 2013, finally got some kind of financial retribution for the property. The new government's attempt at making things right, I guess. My grandfather on my mother's side was a plumber, and since this was a required job in the services industry he was allowed to keep doing it.

On March 21, 1960, in Sharpeville, a township near Johannesburg, thousands of black people converged to demonstrate against the need to carry identity passes. It was supposed to be a peaceful demonstration with the blacks leaving their passes at home and handing themselves in to the police. However, it turned violent and hundreds of people were wounded or killed. The Sharpeville massacre was intrinsic in starting a more brutally run society.

It was no wonder that my parents, as well as some of their siblings, left South Africa in the early sixties. Australia and England were allowing South Africans to immigrate and that is where they dispersed to. What were once two close-knit families with lots of relatives got split up into different countries far away from their home.

When I was traveling the world, at the age of fifty, I went to Australia and spent some time with relatives from my mother's side, my aunt, uncle, and cousins. I learned a lot about my mother's past through stories that were told to me by my aunt and uncle. These stories were relevant to me as they gave me the never-before-heard history of my mother, which allowed me to move forward from forgiving her to understanding what her life was like in order for her to make the decisions she did. This was paramount in my healing journey.

My parents traveled by boat from South Africa to England. My mother was pregnant with my oldest brother, Andre, during this trip so it must have been late 1960. I am not sure where in England they first moved to, but my dad joined the Royal Air Force as an airplane mechanic. He was a perfectionist in his own right, a trait that carried down to his children, albeit good or bad, maybe a little of both as we will see and recognize in this story. My two older brothers were born in England. I am not sure where. Andre was born first, on December 21, 1960, and then, just over two years later, Ashley on March 3, 1963. Andre was born with an incurable illness, aplastic anaemia; Ashley was perfectly healthy. After the birth of Ashley, my father got stationed in a British Air Force base in Changi, Singapore, and on February 9, 1965, I was born. That would be 2 + 9 = 11 and 6 + 5 = 11. I realized the synchronicity of these numbers many years later while meditating at the top of a Mayan temple in Mexico on November 11, 2011, (11.11.11) at 11:11:11. I have two birth certificates, a Singaporean one and a British one, as I was born on a British Air Force base located in Singapore. It was not until fifty years later, while planning my round-the-world trip, when I discovered that Singapore separated from Britain in 1965. Singapore celebrated its fiftieth anniversary the same year as I celebrated my fiftieth birthday.

When I was older, people used to ask me where I was born, and I would proudly say, "Singapore."

They would ask, "Where is that?"

I would reply, "I have no idea."

I always knew that I would go there someday. It was funny; when I was planning my round-the-world trip in 2015, Singapore was not a place I felt I needed to go to. Even when I found out that I could be there for its fiftieth anniversary celebrations, I considered it but still decided not to go. I think it was because Singapore had changed so much since I was born that seeing it again no longer resonated with me.

I purchased a customized round-the-world airline package to take me to all the countries I was going to visit for the first three and a half months as I still needed a bit of security and planning. The last flight ended up in Bali at the end of February, 2016. However, when entering Bali as a tourist you need to show a return ticket within the timelines of the tourist visa, which was thirty days. The cheapest flight out of Bali was to Singapore, go figure. I purchased the Singapore flight thinking that I would not use it. The universe had other plans and I did end up going to Singapore for two or three days. There were no big moments while in Singapore, no recall of memories, but now I can at least say that I did go and visit.

We left Singapore when I was really young to go back to England. I am not sure of the year or how old I was. I have no memories of Singapore, only a few pictures and what I can remember my mother telling me. I know that I had pneumonia at a young age, maybe six months. My dad drove a motorcycle; the house was nice and airy; there was a maid and a gardener. I remember a picture of my brothers fighting in a small pool outside in the garden; a picture of my mother holding me and feeding me my first lychee. From the look on my face I was not impressed. I do not remember anything of my brother's illness back then so I am not sure at what time his illness was discovered.

Our family left Singapore and moved back to England. Our address was 111 Abbey Road, Whitney, Oxfordshire. I remember that address as it reminds me of the Beatles album. I just Googled "Abbey Road" and, surprise, surprise, it was the Beatles' eleventh album. What is it with the number eleven?

We stayed in England until I was seven. That was when we moved to Canada. We moved for Andre as there were better options for medical care in Canada. My memories of England are sparse. I remember Whiskers, our cat. I remember running through Trafalgar Square chasing the pigeons. I have no idea how I know it was Trafalgar Square, I only remember chasing the pigeons and having them all fly away from me. I remember my mother having all her teeth pulled out and me staying beside the bed with her in pain not knowing what to do. I remember our next-door neighbor's children, Sue and Jay. Ashley played with Jay and I played with Sue, who was a couple of years younger than me. A lot later in life, Jan 6, 2014, at 9:04 am (thank you, Facebook messenger, for keeping track of ALL messages), I found Sue and sent her a text message. I also got in touch with Jay and, although we really do not chat, we are all still Facebook friends.

I have faint memories of going to a water park somewhere in England and a parrot pooping on Andre's head. Everyone was laughing and saying that it was good luck. I remember standing outside our tiny fence on the sidewalk and hearing my mother tell her friends to look at me and how spaced out and lost I was. I was always staring off into space. It made me feel picked on and belittled as I was a very shy and introverted little girl, spending lots of time in my anxiety-ridden head.

I remember running through the rain to my ballet class. I loved the class, I loved dancing and I wanted to get there fast. I can hear my mother yelling, "Carla, don't run, you will slip and fall!" I didn't listen, and I ran, and I slipped, and I fell and hit my head on the stone steps going into the building. I was bleeding profusely from a wound located in the middle of my forehead at the third eye. We went to the doctor. He put a bandage on and did not stitch up the cut. I still have a scar from this fall. When I owned *Divine Body*

Spa, my laser machine representative told me he could do laser skin resurfacing to get rid of the scar. I was horrified as the scar is a part of me, I will never remove it. It's funny that I have such a strong feeling about the scar, maybe because it always brought some attention, some care, from strangers wanting to know what happened.

I remember sitting at the dinner table at Christmas time and not being able to leave because I would not eat some kind of yucky green vegetable, I think it was Brussels sprouts. I remember Andre being on experimental drugs for his illness and gaining a lot of weight. I look back now, knowing what I know. I always knew that Andre was sick, terminally ill. But what does that really mean when one is so young? It was just a thing that people said.

I have to say that my younger years in Singapore and England were of the mundane. There was nothing traumatic to speak of. Albeit, my introverted nature was not conducive to having a lot of friends. Family life was family life, except for having a brother who was terminally ill that is. But as a child it was what it was.

CHAPTER 2

1972 to 1974

Move to Canada

When we arrived in Canada, we moved to Gimli, Manitoba. My dad had a job working for an airline there. I remember moving into the house with no furniture. Someone lent us lawn chairs to sit on. We just had the items that we brought on the plane as the rest of our stuff was coming over by boat. I do not remember much more about Gimli. I am not even sure how long we were there before we moved to Winnipeg, Manitoba. I do not think that we were there long as it was summer, or early fall, and we did not go to school there. When we moved to Winnipeg, school had already started and all three of us had to take tests to determine what grades we should be put into, since England's educational system is different from Canada's. We were all about two years apart. So, according to our ages we should have been in Grade 2 (me), Grade 4 (Ashley) and Grade 6 (Andre). However, according to the tests, that is not the way it worked out. I was put into Grade 3, Ashley into Grade 4 and Andre into Grade 5.

In England, I had only learned how to print. I had not yet learned how to read or write cursive. I was extremely introverted and had a very hard time talking to others. On the first day at my new school, I was sitting in class and the teacher wrote something on the blackboard in cursive writing and told us what to do. I sat there terrified and afraid in a new country with no friends and all these strange kids, not knowing what to do. I started crying, tears streaming down my face with a feeling of pure loneliness. The teacher came and talked to me with the entire class watching and listening as I quietly tried to find a voice amid all the fear and anxiety and hopelessness. A whisper emerged to say that I could not read what she had written on the board. I could only read print. I was then taken out and given extra classes to learn how to read and write cursive. In all honesty, I do not remember these extra lessons. There are so many gaps in my history. All I have are glimpses of events.

Although Canada and England both speak English, there is a huge difference in the slang used. When I was in Grade 4, someone had gotten their hair cut and now they had bangs. I had no idea what bangs were, so I assimilated it with a bang from a gun and got really confused - in England they're called fringes. Also, I think it was in Grade 5 when one of the kids was away from school and I heard someone else say that they were playing hooky. I did not know this word, the closest word that I could think of was hockey. That confused me to no end as I could not figure out why someone would be allowed to play hockey during school hours, or who they were playing hockey with as all the kids were supposed to be in school. Hooky is slang for someone who stays away from school without permission. While these times of confusion did not occur on a daily basis, they did lead me further into my head and started a belief that I was no good. My mind always seeing the worst in me.

Since I had moved to England when I was really young, I'd picked up a British accent. For a girl who could barely speak to strangers it was another thing that set me aside when I did say something, as my British accent came out. My friend at the time taught me how to speak Canadian and understand some of the slang. Over time, I lost my British accent. However, there are still words to this day that I have trouble deciding how to pronounce. Garage is one that I still have trouble with.

CHAPTER 3

1974

The Nightmare Begins

The last year or so has been...unpleasant, to say it nicely. My parents fighting all the time. My brother Andre consistently in the hospital, for tests, for new drugs to try, and every time he gets a bruise or a nosebleed. You see, with his illness, his blood does not coagulate so a bruise or a nosebleed could be life threatening. It is hard on me and, I guess, on my other brother Ashley as well. Ashley is the wonder child, always getting straight A's, very handsome, a boy. I, on the other hand, am not so special. There are reasons for this. I am a girl, and girls are not worthy. This is a lesson I have learned from my mother at an early age. I never felt love, compassion or empathy. I was always wrong and causing trouble.

One day, a door-to-door salesman comes to the house. He is selling guitar and accordion lessons. Andre wants to play the guitar; Ashley wants to play the accordion; I want to play the guitar. Andre and Ashley get signed up for lessons and I get told that if they practice and keep up with it, then perhaps I could get lessons ... **I am unworthy.**

I loved dancing and taking ballet lessons in England so, when we get to Canada, I bug and bug and bug my mother to allow me to have lessons. Finally, one day, my mother finds a person who gives lessons in her basement. It wasn't serious, it wasn't fun. I had dreamed of becoming a ballerina and I felt deeply disappointed, **I was not worthy**. I have no idea why my mother did not take me seriously about this as she was a ballerina in her younger years and spoke fondly of it. I want to sing, I like singing, but I am not allowed to take lessons because the boys did not practice their instruments. I go into my bedroom with Andre's guitar book and I sing by myself. I get told to shut up. **I am not good enough, I am not worthy**.

I am going to add something here. An insight from my here and now presence. My mother, back then, was in a new country with three children, one of whom was terminally ill, and a husband who was negligent and whom she fought with a lot. She was also working full-time. I also think that girls in South Africa are not as respected as boys are. Some past beliefs are present for my mother. As I said in my preamble, forgiveness is just a step towards understanding. However, the life lessons that I am learning at this relatively young stage of my life haunt me for my next forty plus years…I am not worthy; I am not good enough; I am less than. Do I feel loved? Nope, not at all. First is Andre, who is sick all the time, then Ashley, who is smart and handsome and athletic, and then I am the last one. All I am is a girl who does not listen. Not much love left for me. Please do understand, these are recollections of my thoughts and feelings at the time. I have done a lot of work to forgive and then to understand.

When I was eight years old, my mother got pregnant; she gave birth to my brother Mark on February 6, 1974. On February 9 of that year I turned nine. In 1973, some relatives from South Africa arrive—Uncle Rex, Auntie Ruth and their kids. Both kids are much older than me. I think Auntie Ruth was a cousin of my mother's. My mother is very happy as she has a friend from home whom she can talk with. We go over there for suppers and visits. My father is still in the picture at that time and he comes as well. My uncle pays special attention to me. I am not used to someone treating me kindly, I am used to being left alone or yelled at. He talks to me, he listens to me, and he takes me downstairs to the basement to show me the ping pong table. He hugs me too long, he tries to kiss me on the lips, he talks dirty to me, he tells me this is our little secret and I am not to tell anyone. I am nine. I have a feeling something is not right, but I am getting attention, attention that I do not get in my home. There is no hugging, there are no kisses, there is no praise, there is only fighting and anger and worrying about Andre and then the pregnancy and then my brother Mark being born.

The trips to the basement when visiting my aunt and uncle become more frequent. There are also special trips to my house when he knows no one is home. Then his penis comes out and I am to touch it, then kiss it and fondle it, and then more dirty stories. I feel uncomfortable, I really do not want to do this, but he is nice to me, he brings me small gifts. He teaches me that **I am worthy of attention if I please him.** I am also not allowed to tell, anyone. It is our secret and I do what he asks.

He is a predator, a known sex offender to little girls. He leaves boys alone. He got chased out of South Africa because of this and my mother knows. Yet she allows him to be alone with me. For if she stood up for me she would lose her only solace, her friendship with Aunty Ruth. I am the offering given freely so my mother can have someone to talk to. I do not find out the information about Uncle Rex being a known pedophile until I am in the midst of post-partum depression after giving birth to my beautifully sweet little baby girl many years later. At that time, I am forced to find the guts to speak out to my family about what happened. The new belief…**I am only good for sexual favors.**

During this time, my father keeps quitting his job or getting fired. You see, he is a perfectionist, and if he feels he is forced to "cut corners" then he quits the job. He goes through different jobs in Winnipeg, then he starts moving towards the west coast, finding and losing jobs along the way. All this is going on while my mother is at home with a new baby and three children, one of those children forever in the hospital. Aplastic anaemia is not a kind illness. But Andre is a fighter. He knows that he will die at an early age. He also has anger, and he doesn't like me very much as I am the cause of turmoil and always fighting with my mother.

Neither one of my brothers is very kind to me. Sibling rivalry, I guess, along with the fact that I am not treated well by my mother, instills the ideas in their heads that I am not worthy. For the most part we ignore each other. If we are not ignoring then we are fighting.

One day, I'm not sure what happened, Andre is nice to me and wants to play board games. I always lose. He wants something. I am nine. He is thirteen. The next thing I remember is being in the downstairs bathroom, naked and out of my body, watching him do things to me. Inserting things in me. But I am not there, I am not in my body. I am floating above, watching, as if it were a movie. A horrible movie. As I am watching what is happening, I am thinking, *This is why he is being nice to me.* He finishes; I get dressed. I am not sure how or why it happened or what transpired to allow it to happen. Lesson affirmed: **You are only good for sexual acts.** At nine years old, I start wetting the bed. Almost every night for at least two to three years. **I am to blame, I am wrong**, it is like I am doing it on purpose. I get shamed and yelled at for doing this.

My mother is overworked. She works a full-time job, has four children to look after, one a baby and one who is terminally ill. Where do I fit in? I don't. She is mad at me all the time because I don't listen to her, I add more work by wetting the bed, and my father is not around. He is in some other city in some other province miles away. My mother calls my father and bitches and screams at him to no end that she cannot control us kids (my brother Ashley and I). He then drives hours to come home to take Ashley and me into the basement to give us the leather belt. I have bruises all over my legs. I go to school and sit in gym class ashamed, looking at the bruises and smelling of pee. This is the love that I get from my father. I have a memory of losing it one day and yelling that I hated him. I then run all over the basement to try to get away as he charges after me with the belt. This is when the other side of the belt gets used—the metal part—as the leather obviously was not doing its trick.

When my father is not at home, which is almost every day, my mother gets so mad at me she has to lash out, to teach me a lesson, to make me behave or some reason like that. She has these old, heavy pots that she cooks in. I think she brought them over with her from South Africa. She breaks the handle of one as she hits it over my head. I have a huge lump on my head as I lie in bed crying while she blames me for breaking her pot.

Another time, she is mad at me again and yells at Ashley to give her something to hit me with. He brings a ruler. It is one of those wooden rulers with a metal edge. She hits me with it and I get a huge fat lip with a cut on it. It is bleeding all over my shirt. The next day, one of her friends is over and she is telling them how I don't listen. She calls me downstairs to show her friend the consequences for my not listening. It is like she is proud of hurting me. I am unsure of her friend's reaction as all I remember is the tremendous hurt, and a bit of anger welling up inside of me.

Is it any surprise that I start thinking about suicide? Is it any surprise that I make a noose in my closet? Is it any surprise that it feels so good when I try to hang myself, when I feel the pressure of the cord around my neck? Oh, how good it feels when I can't breathe. It feels familiar as my breath is taken away from me. These are my prepubescent years. These are the lessons and beliefs that are instilled in my brain, into my being, into my soul...I am not worthy; sex is the only way to get some kind of affection; I am not loved; no one cares about me; I am bad, and the list goes on.

Why did I not actually do it? Why did I stand up and release the pressure when strangling myself? Why am I still alive today? Whilst all of this was happening, I had a deep, instilled feeling that I could not kill myself. I had this huge survival instinct. Even after so much pain and anguish and overcoming, the suicidal thoughts are still there with me. I ponder and do not understand.

My fifty-two-year-old self is sitting in a condo in Playa del Carmen, Mexico, looking out at palm trees blowing in the wind while writing this, and it amazes me how many blank parts of my life I have. How many memories are submerged in my conscious mind. I ask myself, *Do I want to remember? Do I need to remember?* What I do know is that I had a visualization embedded into my being. I am not sure when this started, but it is part of the reason that kept me alive and striving and surviving. This image is of an older me with children in a calm setting, lots of trees and grass and nature. I have a husband who loves me. This image starts when I am young and stays with me through hard times. This image kept me alive, it kept me going and it gave me strength. This image manifested itself when I was in my mid-thirties.

Back to the present. As I am writing the above, I am crying. Tears are pouring from my eyes. Suddenly, I feel that there is something else I need to write, a poem is coming forth. I open a new Word document and the following poem spurts forth onto the paper in the midst of my tears. It takes five minutes to write, and I have never edited it...

Awake in a Nightmare

Awake in a nightmare
I see myself
a pure little child
alone and afraid,
the only solace that I find
is a noose around my neck.

Not being able to speak,
as there is no one to listen,
the lessons I am learning
are not good for the soul.
I am unworthy,
I am bad,
I am wrong.

What a sad little girl
with no one to love her,
she finds strength inside
to lessen the pain.

I am now in my teens
and love is twisted,
if I perform certain acts
someone will care.

But love doesn't work that way
and alone I reside
in the pain that I feel.
I am tossed aside.

My first true love
decides abuse is just fine;
now I am screaming to stop.
"Please don't hit me again."
So in the middle of the night,
in the middle of winter,
I got away and am running
with nothing but a dress
no shoes and no coat.

What am I here for?
What is my purpose
to be in so much pain?
Why am I alive?

There is a strength within me
that just does not go away,
it carries me through,
it keeps me sane.

At fifty-two years of age
I look back and ponder,
I see the poor little child.
I give her my love,
nothing is more deserving
than a pure, innocent babe.

The healing is constant
for there is much to forgive.
I have been told I have a purpose
to let other people know
that no matter how hard life hits you
there is always somewhere to go.

Go deep inside yourself
find the worth that is you;
give the love and attention
to the one that is most worthy,
the authentic you.

My life is far from finished
but it is time I proceed…
with the purpose that has driven me
to help those in need.

To show that there is light
at the end of the tunnel
just listen to your heart
and you too will succeed.

I have read this poem many, many times and each time I read it, I cry. I cry for the lost little girl; I cry for the screwed-up teen; I cry for the abused wife. I cry, and I cleanse, and I feel a deep-hearted compassion and empathy for the person that was me. Each time I read it, and each time I cry, I feel my heart open wider with love. Love not just for me but for all the people who have gone through tragic times. I want to let them know that they are not alone. They have no reason to feel fear or to feel ashamed. They too can let down their mask and allow others to see the truest beauty and strength that resides within.

CHAPTER 4

1978

Becoming a Teenager

The sexual abuse by both my brother and uncle has stopped by the time I am 13. I am not exactly sure when, or why, but it doesn't matter, the damage has been done. The seeds have been planted and watered. The beliefs are now ingrained and beginning to sprout. My head is still full of anxiety, but there is an inner strength, one that lashes out in anger. My mother and I fight all the time now. There is no rest.

I start smoking, I try alcohol, I try marijuana; I find that I have a voice when under the influence. My introvert gets pushed aside and a mask gets put on. A mask that allows me to speak and be funny. It is a relief from the pain and anger residing at home.

I am now 13 and entering womanhood. My body is changing; I get my period. I notice one day as I wipe myself after having a pee that there is blood on the toilet paper. I know what this is because we learned about it in school. I become afraid, but I can't tell my mother. I feel ashamed. I wad up some toilet paper and put it in my panties.

I do this for a couple of days and then my mother storms into my room and shouts at me. "I found blood on the toilet seat! Do you have your period?" I sit on my bed ashamed, saying nothing as she yells at me. "When were you going to tell me? Do you know what this means?"

I silently whisper, "Yes."

My mother yells, "OK, so tell me what this is!" I don't answer. I feel small. I feel like I am trapped in a hole and she keeps yelling to tell her what it is. I have no idea why she is so angry about this.

I say, "We learned about it in school." This answer does not appease her. She keeps yelling, trying to force me to tell her what having a period is all about. She gets frustrated and goes and grabs the encyclopedia, throws it at me, and tells me to read it and to come and explain it back to her when I figure out what it means. Then she storms out of my room. I curl up into a fetal position and lay there on my bed. I cry and feel sorry for myself. When I cry myself out, I get out my curling iron and make the noose in my closet. It's time to find release. Today, I understand that the choking was a physical reaction for not being able to tell my truth, for not having a voice; I still get that tight feeling around my neck in certain circumstances.

I fight with my mother all the time. At one point I decided to do something nice for her, so I got up early and started ironing all the clothes and sheets. It took me a long time, but I was proud and happy and looking forward to her thanks. When she came home and saw it, she said, "It's nice to see that you can do this, so now it is a part of your chores." No, "Thank you," no nice words. I feel crappy, yet again. Now, instead of the noose, I decide to take pills. I sit at the table alone and cry and eat Tylenol. One at a time. I am not sure how many I took, but I finally exhausted myself from crying and fell asleep with my head on the kitchen table. It is fairly obvious that I did not take enough to kill myself, but I was oh so sick for a while. No one ever knew or saw any of the attempts that I had made on my life. This was my secret.

CHAPTER 5

1978 to 1981

Life with my Father

At some point, my mother decides it would be best if I spend some time with my father. It will get me out of the house as I am nothing but a thorn in her side. I think it was at thirteen that the first visit to my father happened. He had worked his way from Winnipeg, MB, through Alberta, and was now living in Williams Lake, British Columbia. It is funny how an absent parent who is only home to beat you looks like the better option. I travel over to him, and because I was so young my mother sent Andre with me as this was during one of his stable times. Andre is not pleased. He resents having to go with me. I can feel the anger and hatred as we travel. By bus? By train? I have no recollection. He is mad as he doesn't want to be with me on this journey and all I do is cause harm and unrest at home. The sexual abuse has stopped before this. Now he is just mad at me all the time. In any case, I get there, and my dad is staying in the basement of some people. He is getting free accommodation as he works on fixing up their basement. They have a daughter about the same age as me, so we spend our time together. I don't really see my father. My time is spent with the daughter. She is beautiful and wild and exciting. We hitchhike; we go to parties; we have fun; it is too brief; it's only been a couple of weeks. Then I have to go back to Winnipeg. I return by myself because Andre's job was just to take me there.

Nothing has changed at home, except that I am becoming a bit wilder. I run away from home. I stay out all night at parties. I meet this guy and hang out at his place. His mother is on welfare and he has dropped out of school. But we make out and he treats me well, and the drugs and alcohol help take me away from the pain. It also helps hide my shyness, because it allows me to pretend to be someone else by putting on a mask. My past lessons are being reaffirmed: you are only worthy of sexual acts. That is how I find attention. That is how I find someone to care—well, what I think is care—about me. It's a twisted sense of reality that allows more layers of hurt and pain to be laid upon the deep set core ideas that were placed on me early on in life.

As I finish up my writing for the day, a poem is shouting to be let out…

Finding Love

Out there alone
an introvert at heart
with the life lessons learned
deep in my soul.

Not worthy,
not good,
I am nobody,
no one cares,
I have to find love.

To have a touch that is not harsh,
kind words that caress,

a feeling of oneness
deep inside my chest.

A fleeting moment of heart
opened up to the soul
only to find out
that is not enough.

My open heart
searching for more
keeps finding falseness
to be used once more.

Again and again
I try ever so hard
if I am the best
then maybe I can be worthy
of someone's true love.

No matter how many times
the lesson is learned
my heart stays open
but yet again to be burned.

I know deep inside
I am worthy,
I am true,
someone just needs to see
the beauty that resides within me.

The compassion and empathy
are needing to be released

to let go and allow
the heart to be free.

The strength and the knowing
that I am worthy
is drowned by the neediness
that resounds through my body,
the neediness that is felt
as soon as one comes near,
it blinds them with fright
so they leave me in fear.

Alone I sit
once again in tears.
What is wrong with me now?
Why cannot someone see
the deep passion and love
I am wanting to give?
For what I give
may come back to me.

It takes many years
to discover the truth
the love that I need
is within my own being.
To truly be loved by another
one needs to love oneself first.

I am still in awe and amazement at the poetry that is being released as I write my memoirs.

The next time I get sent to my dad he is in Sandspit, Queen Charlotte Islands. I am pretty sure I am traveling alone. It is in the summer and I am fourteen. Sandspit is on a tiny island off the coast of northern BC. My dad has a small place, not very nice, pretty rough actually. Even though I am still introverted, I do meet a girl and she shows me around. We party with some people. She shows me where magic mushrooms grow naturally, and there are a bunch of us picking mushrooms. Then later there is a party and we all have mushrooms. There is a boy and he likes me, I am not sure what to do with this. I take away the fear and anxiety by drinking, taking mushrooms and smoking pot. One of my lessons in life: sex gives attention. It doesn't take a rocket scientist to know what happened. The next day, the mask is removed, for with no substance abuse I turn into the introvert that I am at heart. I barely say a word; my anxiety-ridden mind is blank, it does not know what to say. The boy is confused, wondering, *Where did the vibrant young girl go?* Of course, my father is nowhere to be seen. Visiting him is like living alone. No parenting; no caring; no loving embrace. As long as I stay out of his way it is OK. He is still handsome and has an easy time getting girlfriends and that is where he spends his time. He is selfish, and I am just in the way, so he leaves me to my own devices. I have no idea if my mother knows about his girlfriends.

I go back home to Winnipeg. At home, life is as it always has been, fighting all the time with my mother and being unhappy. At thirteen I started getting into trouble, hanging out with the wrong people, smoking, a little alcohol, a little drugs. Nothing extreme, but out there in the world, in an introverted soul with the life lessons ingrained deep into my being, I am looking for love—in all the wrong places. My wanton ways lead to more anger from my mother as I have now become uncontrollable.

Shortly after I leave Sandspit, my father moves once again, there is no more land to go west so he goes north to Fort Smith, NT. I arrive in the summer of my fifteenth year. My father has an apartment; I never see him. I am alone again. I go to school; I am now in Grade 11. I hang out with the wrong people and party and get used. Except, this time, I contract gonorrhea. I had no idea what was wrong, so I left it for a long time. In the end, the pain was so bad that I had to leave school. I went back to the apartment and laid on the floor clutching my lower abdomen. I couldn't move. I am alone. There is no one to help. I cry out in pain. I yell for help. No one is coming. I pass out for a bit.

When I wake, the pain is not as bad and I stumble to the hospital where they admit me right away. I was in the hospital all weekend. By myself. I am assuming that the hospital must have called my dad to let him know where I was. But I don't remember seeing him there. I was told the infection was so severe that I might not ever be able to have a baby. There was probably scarring that was going to affect my Fallopian tubes. I was OK with this, because why would I want to bring a baby into this world? I was definitely not the mothering or nurturing type. I did not know how to be that as it was never given to me.

There are no groceries in the house, I have no money, and my father is with his girlfriend all the time. I am not allowed over to her house as I am told she does not like me. You see, Fort Smith is a small town, and rumors spread fast, especially about a new girl who doesn't have a clue how to say no. My lesson early in life about being treated nicely for sex is losing its power as being treated nicely only lasts until the sex. Then there is nothing after that. Before it was repetitive; now it is just being used for one time. I am lost and confused and alone.

I get sent back to Winnipeg to visit my mother. I am not sure what time of year it is. I remember my dad sending me a ticket to go back to Ft. Smith. My mother gets into a fight with him and cancels the ticket. I honestly think it is because of them fighting, it had nothing to do with either one of them wanting me. I was a pawn in their game. Every time he sends a ticket, she cancels it. I am devastated as I cannot live with my mother. I am heartbroken. He sends me a ticket on the sly, and I pack my stuff and call a cab. My little brother Mark sees this and calls my mother who goes and cancels the ticket again. Last attempt; I have to sneak out of the house, past my brother and not let anyone know. I am home-free and away I go. My father promises never to send me back to my mother again. My mother is livid and yells at my father over the phone, but there is nothing she can do.

The following poems was written on September 1, 2017...a few days after actually writing about the experience. I guess there were still things that needed to come out, that needed to be said, that needed to be expressed.

STD

I was fifteen,
just a young teen
looking for love
in all the wrong places.

I contracted
a disease,
not a clue;
I left it too long.
Lying in the middle
of the living room
screaming for help,
not able to move.

The pain was horrendous,
there was no one to help me

so I stumbled alone
to emergency.

A weekend alone
getting treatment.
Where was my dad?
No one knew.

There I am,
just a young teen
being told
it would be a miracle
if I ever have a baby.

I don't think
I ever did
comprehend
what I was told.

Alone and lonely
with no one to help.
The strength inside me
allowed me to see
that I only had myself
to stand beside me.

And the poetry continues to spurt forth...

Sperm Donor

Sperm donor
that is what you are;

that is what you have become
to me.

The only time I see the word
Love
is in an extravagant birthday card,
"Love Graham."

Is that supposed
to make it all right?
All those days and nights
without a father.

When I see you
It's for a trip to the basement,
the nightmare of running
and screaming
and getting beaten
by a leather belt.

If you make him angrier
the buckle will be used,
it hurts so much more
than the leather
you see.

The marks it makes
are quite clear
on my legs
and in my soul.

Fear and rage,
anger and hatred,

that is what comes out
in the middle of the basement.

Then away you go
off to your next job,
moving miles away
so you don't have to be
face to face
with what you have done.

Oh, the lessons I learned
in my teens
took many years
to settle and clear.

Now I am me,
my authentic being.
I learned to forgive
but forget
oh no.

Sperm donor you are
and always will be,
for the love
that a daughter should have
for her father
is lost in the physical and mental abuse
from so many years before.

I have learned to let go
of that need to be loved
by the one who helped make me
so long ago.

You never had
the capacity or knowledge
to be a father,
of that I am sure.

The regret and the sorrow
that you now feel
is so selfish
as it is still
all about you.

How can one have anger at
someone so naive?
So a sperm donor you are
I do believe.

The anger dissipates
the sorrow clears
as a fuller understanding
of what you are
permeates my being.

I no longer take it personally.
My strength is clear
as my inner being knows
my worthiness and more.

CHAPTER 6

1981 to 1983

Alone and in Edmonton

I turn sixteen and finish Grade 11. It is summer now. My dad and I had a positive conversation about me living there and I had hopes that things would get better, that we could be closer. One of my girlfriends, Karen, talks to me and tells me that she is moving to Edmonton to stay with a friend of hers and was wondering if I wanted to go with her. I told her no, because my dad and I were getting along much better. I think this was a Monday that we had the conversation.

On the Saturday, I am woken up by my father yelling at me. "Get out of bed, get your bags packed, you have two hours and I am putting you on a plane and sending you back to your mother!"

I am confused and sleepy and not sure what is going on. I ask, "Why?"

He says, "The rumors going around about you are affecting my girlfriend, and I cannot have you living here anymore." It was true. There were rumors about me sleeping around and partying. I know deep in my heart that I cannot go back to Winnipeg, cannot go back and live with my mother. It would be the end of me.

I take the flight from Fort Smith to Edmonton, and then stay there. I do not use the rest of the ticket. I find a phone and I call my girlfriend Karen. She will be coming down to Edmonton in a week. I sit at the airport and wait. I am not sure what to do. I have no money. I have nowhere to go. I sleep at the airport.

It didn't feel right to contact my mother or my father when I decided to stay in Edmonton. Two to three weeks later, I finally decide to call my mother so that she can stop worrying about me. You see, I know that my mother would call my father and start some sort of fight with him if I went back to Winnipeg. Or maybe my father would make a call to make sure I got home OK. In any case, I was feeling bad about making them worry. I call my mother, and she had no idea that my dad had sent me away. Another dagger in the heart. No one knew; no one cared. *I am not worthy,* keeps resounding in my being. *You are not wanted, you are not loved. Fuck both of you!* my pain screams. *I have no one,* resounds from my soul. Oh, what a troubled life I lead. I decide not to call either one of them for a couple of months after this.

The next morning, after sleeping at the airport, a skycap came by to talk with me. A skycap is a person who helps someone with their luggage. He tells me that security is watching me and will be coming over soon to find out why I am all alone in the airport and not going anywhere. I tell him what is going on. He says that he has an apartment in the south end of town. He works nights and sleeps days and says that I would be welcome to stay there until Karen arrives. He is trustworthy and keeps his promise. He does not try anything with me. A sigh of relief.

Karen comes to town and we reunite. We take a taxi to her friend's place. Her friend is a single mother with a newborn baby and she is on welfare. It is a sparse, one-bedroom apartment with no food in the house. There is construction happening on the roof of one of the apartment buildings across from ours. Hot looking men with their shirts off. We go out on the balcony and flirt from a distance. Three of them come over with some beer and we party for a while. I can't remember the name of the girl we are staying with. Anyways, she ends up with one of the guys in her bedroom. Karen goes to the bathroom with her male friend and I am with my companion in the living room. The couch is a foldaway bed. I am not sure what happened with the relationships of the other two. But the guy I am with likes me and continues seeing me. My first real boyfriend.

He is French Canadian and lives out of town in a house in the country with his family. He takes me to his place and I meet his large extended family. They are really nice and get along well together. I am still very shy and do not say much. I live in my head with my voice still locked inside me. But they like me. One of his sisters pierces my ears with ice and a needle, with a potato behind my ear so the needle stops when she pokes it through. I keep the thread in my ears while it heals. I still have the same piercing today.

He treated me well with kindness and compassion. I am not sure what happened. Probably my fault as I don't know what to do with someone who treats me well and who is not using me. I still don't know how to talk, I have mixed feelings. *I am not worthy; it won't last.* I am in a constant state of confusion. Not knowing what I am feeling or how to talk. The mask fails, and I have no idea what I am doing. A constant state of anxiety. We stopped seeing each other after a month or so. I know it was me, running away scared. The first to leave so that I don't get hurt.

I need to find a job, I have no money. Who will hire a sixteen-year-old with a Grade 11 education and no work experience? It is hard. I travel everywhere by foot and by bus. I get turned away a lot. I finally find a place that will hire me. It is a cafeteria in downtown Edmonton in a government building. I help prepare sandwiches and work the cash register. My manager is a very kind lady, she is older, maybe in her sixties. We get to know each other, and she likes me. I now have a little bit of money and I get to take home the leftover, expired sandwiches, so I have something to eat. I also steal packets of peanut butter so I can eat on the weekends. My manager sees something in me. Potential I guess. She talks to one of the regular customers to see if I can get a job working for the government. I get an interview and I get the job. I am now a file clerk for the government. I work in Petroleum Plaza in downtown Edmonton. I pull files for the government workers and deliver them by cart. There are two towers in the building, so I do a lot of walking from tower to tower and floor to floor delivering files.

I move away from Karen and her friend as I have more money now. I am not sure where I move to. During the time I was in Edmonton, I lived in many different places, moving every three to six months. It is easy to move as I do not own anything other than clothes. I keep moving because I am not settled in myself or in my life. I keep trying to find a place that feels comfortable, not knowing that the discomfort is coming from within not from my external surroundings. I am lost. My mother knows, by this time, that I will not be going back to her in Winnipeg, and my father, well he has his girlfriend and doesn't really care.

I go to the bar on the weekends. I get in 99 percent of the time, although I am just sixteen. I look older than I am. My brother Ashley comes for a visit. He drives his motorcycle up from Winnipeg to Edmonton. I am proud of him, he has made a life. He is strong and powerful, and we have fun together. We go to a bar to see a band. I am a little tipsy, so my fun self comes out. I have many different personalities, you see, as I have no idea who I am. I am not whole, I am split. The main personality is in my head with no voice, afraid and shy and ridden with anxiety. Going to the bar and drinking allows the fun personality to come out, which is not afraid and can talk to people. I ask the band to play a song for my brother. After the band has finished, the drummer comes over, his name is James. He is twenty-six years old. My next boyfriend. Once again, I get treated well. We stay together for a year or two. It is the destructive voices inside my soul that make me leave. The unworthiness, the needing more, the neediness, I am not sure.

At the end of this sentence you can see a poem coming out. Here are the three poems that emerged after the last sentence…

True Love

To find true love
that is the goal,
to have one see
deep inside my soul.

But I have lost my voice,
don't know how to speak.
If I tell the truth
someone will freak.

The truth is not kind,
it made me unworthy,
it sits in my body,
an unwanted guest
that keeps knocking at the door.

So many secrets to hide.
Pretend to be someone else,
put on the mask.
What's inside is not pretty;

no one wants to hear
the forbidden stories
that make me feel fear.

Hide away, hide away,
become someone else
as you have learned at a young age
you are no good as yourself.

When love comes knocking,
you may open the door
but only a little
as you cannot handle more.

You ignore and conceal
but the truth is always there.
The more you hide it
the stronger it gets,
so when you least expect
it comes out with a vengeance.

All that you have felt
all you feel now
comes out to project
on the love that you found.

Self-sabotage it's called,
how does one stop
to be so mean and angry
to the one that you love?

That was the lesson
I learned young in life

to love is to hurt
and so I suffice.

The learning to change
to open up and see
the wicked life lessons
that were burned into me.

A lot of anguish
self-sacrifice and more
to open those wounds
and learn a new life
that is in store.

So hence I do come from
a life torn to shreds
to put it back together
to release the anger and hate.

To understand fully
that the life once led
is not the here and now
and needs to be put to bed.

The change is slow in coming,
it does take some time
to go through the grief
and give myself mine.

The loving that was not there
comes from deep in my soul,
the blaming that I put forth
is now tranquil and silent

as I have replaced it
with love and compassion.

I am now on the road
on the journey to see
the real authentic me
in all my glory.

Love and compassion abound,
I find the empathy
deep within and sound
to be able to give to others
what I now give to self.

So when you read this story,
know it to be true
that there is light at the end of the tunnel
and that light is you!

Love in a Bar

Finding love in a bar
ten years my senior,
he treats me right,
he treats me well,
he likes the mask;
I hide me well.

A year and a half later
I am not happy,
it is the destructive voices
inside my soul
that make me leave.

The unworthiness,
the needing more,
the neediness,
I am not sure.

My search for love
ends up useless
as I am unable to accept.
I am worthless.

I am too young
to understand
the damage that has been done
the damage that still stands.

So I leave a love
still in my mask
to look for more,
"More what?" I ask.

An empty hole
needs to be filled
but with what
I have no clue.

So alone again
I search the world
looking external
for what I withhold.

It takes many years
to discover the truth.
As I look back

I see the hurt
the pain,
the searching,
the hope,
the fear.

To have someone complete me,
take away the wounds
love me so deeply
that I can be me.

I have found that person,
they were with me all along.
Instead of looking outwards
I look internal
and the love
it is found.

For who will love you more
than you and yourself?
Find the compassion within you
and you will feel
the overpowering worthiness
that was lost
in between.

Introvert

A lonely introvert
unable to speak,
lost in thoughts,
no voice to be heard.

A lonely existence
with nothing to say
except the persistent mind
getting in the way.

To have someone talk to you
and not have words come out,
the mind going blank,
mouth not moving,
fear comes about.

What do I do now?
I nod and say nothing,
hoping they will disappear,
hoping I will disappear.

They move along
and my mind screams;
do not leave,
my mouth is in tears.

How to overcome
this deadly fear?
I move along to the back wall
and disappear.

Alcohol and drugs
help me find my voice,
I am witty and funny
the belle of the ball.

The strength inside me
says I am worth more,
no more substance abuse,
I must go it alone.

I must find the voice
that was lost in my youth
for someone just may hear
the wisdom that I hold.

Let go of the fear,
let your mind go clear,
just answer the question,
do not freeze in fear.

It takes such a long time
to find a way
to get the words out,
put the mind at stay.

The authentic you
has such wisdom and clarity.
They are not better than you,
you do have something to say.

Love and compassion
I give to myself
to let my tongue loose
to speak with my voice.

Let go of the past beliefs.
The past that hurts so much

made you feel inadequate
to lose voice and touch.

You are wise beyond your years
and people need to hear
what you have to say
loud and clear.

CHAPTER 7

1984

Pushing my Boundaries

I am now nineteen and I come to a realization that I am not going to survive in this world as an introvert. To push my boundaries, I put myself in situations that make me talk to people. I am now renting a suite in a basement of a house and still working for the government as a file clerk. I become friends with the owner of the house, Gerry, his brother, Sean, and another girl who is living in the main house with them. We party and hang out. It was a good time.

Gerry introduces me to a friend of his. His name is Gerry as well. He is a skydiver, and has just been featured on the front page of the *Edmonton Sun*, which is a local daily newspaper. It was a picture of him skydiving. We talk and hang out and date for a couple of weeks. He asks me if I want to be a 'Sunshine Girl'. Every day they feature a different girl inside the paper. She is called the 'Sunshine Girl". I nervously say OK, as I know this will help overcome my introverted personality, and he makes a call to the photographer that took his cover photo. The next thing I know, I am in the photo studio getting pictures done. I am terrified. I hardly say a word. I can't make up my mind what to wear. I am horrendously anxious. I listen to the photographer's instructions and end up surviving the photo shoot. It is a couple of weeks before the paper comes out with me as the 'Sunshine Girl'. August 14, 1984, is the exact date. I go out and buy as many copies of the paper as I can. I go to work. I deliver files in the two towers and people are stopping me and commenting on the picture. I am shy and I don't know what to say. But at the same time, I am proud and happy with all the attention that I get. Oh, how the mind works, one part proud and the other part saying you are not worthy, you are not good, the attention is not for you. I do not know how to say thank you or accept a compliment, so I look away or I look down and say nothing. This is a paramount time in my life as I am internally pushing myself to go out and get exposure in order to release myself from the introverted jail I have been living in. At the same time, it is a nightmare for me, and my voice is still quiet and says nothing. My mind is in turmoil.

Gerry also teaches skydiving. I am deathly afraid of heights. However, my inner strength pushes me and I spend a weekend taking lessons. I do two static line jumps; this is where they pull the cord for you. Then my third jump is a buddy jump. There are three of us in the plane, two instructors and I. The first instructor goes out of the plane and hangs on the strut. Then I go out and hang from the strut while the second instructor is inside the plane. He counts to three and we all let go at the same time. This is a true free fall, as the instructors' jobs are to fly beside me and make sure that I am doing what it is I am supposed to do, which is check my altimeter and pull the chord at the right height. I do it. It is scary and exhilarating at the same time. Shortly after, Gerry and I stop seeing each other as my shyness got the best of me and he found someone else who was also a skydiver.

Gerry, who is my landlord, has another friend, Marcel. Marcel is cute and muscular and a lot of fun. I feel comfortable with him and we become friends. We slept together once, but there is something in the back of my mind saying that this is not wise. I am finding my voice to say no. He respects this and, while we do sleep in the same bed on occasion, we do not have sex. It feels good just to be with someone without thinking that I need to give it up. He tells me about this houseboat trip that he is going on in Shuswap Lake, a beautiful lake in southern BC that is famous for houseboating. I get a ticket and we go together. Everyone buys food and drinks and we get on the boats. It has been a long day. We start drinking. Marcel and I have purchased a bottle of Baileys, a bottle of Kahlua and a bottle of Grand Marnier. I start doing shots, one from each bottle. I get really drunk and pass out in the bed on the houseboat we rented. I wake and the boats are all parked on the beach. No one is aboard our boat. I start walking down to the beach. I run into some people and start drinking again. I get drunk and decide to visit each fire on the beach and introduce myself. I make many friends. The mask is on again and the shyness gone. The next day, I wake and everyone is saying hello. I don't remember anyone and am lost. You see, the alcohol takes away the introvert. However, once the alcohol is gone, the introvert is back and very, very shy. It really is not a good combination going from extrovert one moment to introvert the next. No wonder I am so alone and lonely. No one knows how to take me. I am a dichotomy.

There are people learning how to water ski. I decide to give it a try. The guy who is teaching is very cute. We find each other later and hook up. He was very nice. We have a wonderful night in the houseboat I am staying in. In the morning, I lose my ability to talk. I have nothing to say. I don't know what to say. The words are stuck in my throat and my mind has shut down. This is probably why nothing else happened.

It is later that year, in the fall, that I see an ad in the paper looking for people to be extras in a local movie production. Another chance to come out of my shell. I call, book an appointment, and show up at the auditions. I meet the guy who is casting the extras. He says that he has a feature extra part in the movie for me, but has to see my body before he decides. He asks me to take my dress off, I can leave my panties and bra on. This is legit. I have a bra, no panties but pantyhose on. He comes in with a woman to make me feel safe, which calmed me a little, and then says yes, I have the part. They will call me with details. I am living in Edmonton in shared accommodation at this time with this weird guy, Arnold. I am told that in one of the scenes I am massaging the leading actor. Arnold says he will teach me how to massage. He is creepy. I get uncomfortable vibes from him. My intuition says, "Stay away." I listen to this feeling and make excuses not to.

The day of the shoot, I get picked up at home and taken to a house somewhere. It has an inside pool, and this is where the shooting of the day will take place. There are lots of people, all dressed in bathing suits. I have brought two suits with me, a gold lame string bikini and a white bikini. The name of the movie is *Birds of Prey* by Trapped Productions, and it was released in 1985. I have two scenes, one with the gold lame string bikini. I am serving the actors drinks at a poolside table. In the second scene I am wearing a white bikini bottom and a scarf made into a top. It is in this scene that I am sitting beside the lead actor with another girl on the other side, and we are massaging his arms. Later on, I was told that the scarf fell off one of my boobs during shooting. Thank God they edited that part out. I am desperately shy and say nothing all day, all this work to speak to people, to get out of my head and I am still at a loss. I am told that one of the men in the crew is interested in me, maybe wants to take me on a date. I still say nothing. I get taken home and do not hear from him again. Why oh why do I put myself into these situations to see myself fail so miserably? The main thing is that I need to get out of myself, to start speaking to people, and I have to try. I need to survive, I need to try. It was quite a few years later, when living in St. Albert with my husband and children, that I found a copy of this movie in the local movie store. I was also told that it aired on late night TV.

I get tired of working for the government. I am bored, even though I finally have a good income and some savings. You see, there is an inherent quality inside me that needs to save money, to never go into debt. I do this, I save, and don't spend. I also miss out on opportunities. There is a constant stream of thoughts going through my head, and now it includes, *You cannot afford it. You don't have enough money.* How the hell did that belief get in there? To trace it back, I think the root cause is the "I am not worthy" repertoire that constantly goes on. I quit my job with the government and go work as a coat checker at Denny Andrews American Bar. Denny Andrews is a brand new nightclub, one of the hottest places in Edmonton at the time. The Edmonton Oilers go there a lot, and this is in their heyday when they are winning all the time. Mark Messier was a constant, but I have also seen Wayne Gretsky there.

I decide that I need to get my Grade 12 equivalency test (GED) so that I can get a decent job as I am now nineteen. As the chances of getting something good with only a Grade 11 education would be very hard. I study while working as a coat checker at Denny Andrews. I get my Grade 12 GED on the first try. Whew, that hump was over. I am bored at Denny Andrews as working at the bar was not something I wanted to do for life. I felt like there was not much left for me in Edmonton, so after my twentieth birthday, I left to go back to Winnipeg, to my mothers house. Me being away for so many years has allowed our relationship to become closer, and I now feel comfortable going back home. This is a typical behavior of mine. Always moving, always relocating. I am searching for something, for somewhere where I feel at home, feel safe, and where I can feel at peace. I was constantly looking and searching externally, not realizing that I needed to look internally, not realizing that I needed to change my conditioning, my thinking, my belief system. Once again, I have a strength that tells me I am worthy and that there is something out there for me, while at the same time having the chant of unworthiness now deeply ingrained into every pore of my body. A consistent internal fight.

CHAPTER 8

1984

Andre Passes

This chapter should actually be inserted into the previous chapter as it happened while I was working for the government and before Denny Andrews. However, it is an important part of my life and deserves its own chapter.

I was nineteen and it was November, 1984. I get a call from home, Andre, who was twenty-three, is in the hospital and he is not doing well. I had saved enough money that I could book a flight back to Winnipeg. I visit him in the hospital, my brother who molested me and then had such anger for me. We had never talked about the past, or in general really. I don't really know this person who is lying on the hospital bed. I start talking and I tell him that my car is not doing well. He started asking me questions about the car and then telling me what to do to fix it. It was the first real conversation that we have ever had. This, I felt, was his way of saying that he cared. He could not say it outright. But I felt it, I knew it, deep down I knew. I stayed a couple of days and his health was not changing. I had to go back to work. I left and went back to Edmonton. A couple of weeks later, I got a call that he passed, it was just before his twenty-forth birthday. It was like an out-of-body experience. I was watching what was going on from a distance, unable to understand. That night I went out to a bar by myself. I bought some pills from someone at the bar, no idea what they were, but something like ecstasy—I never take pills—I take three or four of them. I am wasted. I don't know how but I got home safe. The next day, I am exhausted. I am coming down from the pills. It did the job. It numbed me enough so that I could not think.

Ashley bought me a ticket back to Winnipeg for the funeral as I had spent my savings on the ticket to go see Andre in the hospital a week or so before. My mother goes to see the body. I do not want to. I don't want to remember Andre lying there in a coffin. I prefer to remember him alive. My final memories are of Andre, finally, after all these years, talking to me, not looking down at me with anger, but trying to help me. I believe that he was asking for forgiveness so that he could pass, letting me know that he did care for me. The entire funeral was surreal. People talked to me, gave me their condolences. I cried a lot. I had no idea what was going on. I left Winnipeg to go back to Edmonton. I was still in a daze. It was shortly after that when I left the government to work at Denny Andrews and got my GED. At this point, my torrid past of sexual abuse was still a secret.

Below are two poems that emerged when writing about my brother's death. The poems need a bit more context in order to truly understand what is being said. Spirituality had entered my realm when I was thirty-nine, so the energy rushes and instinctual feelings I write about were already prevalent in my life. On the morning of December 21, 2010, I was driving to my business, Divine Body Spa. It was the middle of winter in Edmonton, Alberta Canada. It was cold, and the sky was clear. As I was driving, I was talking to my mother on the phone and, suddenly, a rainbow appeared. At the same time, I felt a huge energy rush go through my body and I started to cry. I hung up the phone and pulled over to the side of the road. I sat there for a while, trying to pull myself together. I drove to the spa and called my mother to let her know what happened. I knew it was the winter solstice that day, but she also reminded me that it was Andre's birthday. As soon as she said that, another energy rush went through my body and I knew it to be true. It was Andre giving me a sign that he was there and watching out for me. I will go into this occurrence a bit deeper in a later chapter.

Born to Be Gone

To live a life
knowing that you will die,
not knowing when,
not understanding why.

A life taken at any time
is a sorry feeling
for all around.

But to know that your passing
is because of an illness,
you will not live long
as there is no cure.

That is my brother,
born to be gone.
I don't know how
he lasted so long.

Full of anger
for me alone.

What did I do
to cause such harm?

On his hospital bed
he lays so weak,
not the brother I know
he starts to speak.

"What is wrong with your car?"
he whispers to me.
"I can help you with that,"
he offers freely.

This is his way
of telling me
that he loves me,
he does
and he needs me to know.

I feel the energy,
the forgiveness he has.
I forgive as well
so that he can pass.

He is now with me,
I feel it deep.
He has shown me signs
so that I believe.

I love you, my brother,
I forgive all that was done.
I feel your soul,

you are with me forever.
Forever I behold.

My Brother

I hear of your passing,
I am in a state
of sorrow,
of heartache,
of pain,
of disbelief.

I knew my entire life
that you would pass early
but wasn't it just
a horrible story?

The medications,
the hospitals,
the experimental drugs
all seemed so normal
as if that was life.

How does a small child
process the fact
that her brother will only
be in her life for a short time?

The reality hits home,
the last visit in the hospital.
Oh what time was wasted
on the normal mundane

of living life,
it was insane.

It is what it is;
It was what it was.

I look back now
and forgive what was done
for the life you lived
was not a normal one.

I thank you so much
for reaching out to me
many years later;
in a rainbow you came,
showering me with energy
on a cold winter day.

It was the day of your birth,
the winter solstice I know,
that you gave me such love
and I knew I was not alone.

I thank you, my brother,
for showing me
that your soul is still alive
and looking out for me.

CHAPTER 9

1985 to 1987

Back to Winnipeg and First Marriage

When I got back to Winnipeg I started working for the Waterbed Gallery. Even with my GED, getting a job is hard. My resume is sparse; cafeteria help, file clerk, and coat checker does not leave one with many options. Sales, it seems, is the only occupation that is within my reach. I excel at sales, my mask is much improved. My introverted self is still residing strongly inside myself. But it has been slightly overcome by my need to survive, and so the mask gets placed and does its job. The Waterbed Gallery expands and opens a second location, the Bedroom Gallery. I am the person that they ask to be manager. Really! Me?

It is a drive that I have in myself for being the best that I can be, maybe a bit of a perfectionist, a trait inherent in my father. I get bored of working at the Bedroom Gallery, once again a trait that my father has, not being able to stay at a job long. Normally, my work history is to start at the lowest step on the ladder, work my way up to management within two years, then get bored, quit my job and start looking for something else. It makes me wonder if this is such a good trait. I terminate my position at the Bedroom Gallery and look for another job.

OMG here we go again, I am looking for a job. I am having a hard time finding something. I start working for Kirby vacuum cleaners selling door to door. I meet this man who is working there. His name is Albert. He woos me and I go home with him. I sleep with him—well, because that's what I do. He lives in a basement in some sketchy neighborhood. He becomes a "manager" with his own van of people selling vacuums door to door. He drops us off at different streets as we knock on houses. I am not very good. I do not sell much. He is good. I find out later that he knows how to lie very well. We move to Saskatoon, SK to set up a new location. We get cats and dogs and have a place close to the river. We get married about a year after we met. I ask my brother Ashley to give me away. My father is not happy with not giving me away, so he stays away. That is fine with me.

Life is fleeting. Sometimes good, mostly not so good as I see the abusive behavior sneak up and I start seeing glimpses outside of the mask of the person I call my husband.

The following poem came out of me after writing the above. I notice that these poems, which channel through me as I write, are very cathartic. It is a release for me. As I write, I allow myself to feel fully what has happened, and with that I am able to release the negative energy that has been stored inside my being…for years. It is like peeling an onion, one layer at a time. I find that my deepest layers come from my earliest experiences. All of my experiences are layered over the top of the deep-seated lessons I learned early on in life. I have not yet, at this point in time of my life, experienced any spiritual awakening or growth, so I am not aware of the patterns, of the lessons, of the beliefs that were ingrained into my being. It is kind of like living in a perpetual abusive pattern. Never learning, pushing down all the pain, creating layer after layer of hurt and pain, each one exponentially adding to the layers of the onion. And yet, there is a strength in me. A strength that will not let me give up. A strength that says there is more to me than what I am receiving. A strength of knowing that if I keep trying it will all work out.

Abuse

I meet a man wanting
to have me in his life,
he makes me feel special,
wants to make me his wife.

We move to another place,
we make a home,
we say our vows
and now we are one.

I want to give him everything,
heart and soul,
the need in me is sated
for a while I suppose.

After a year
of being wed
another man enters
into my bed.

This man has hatred and anger,
something he learned from his past
as he saw his father
beat his mother,
it's his life lessons holding fast.

It starts out slowly
with a harsh word or two
escalating faster
with the physical abuse.

He is so sorry
that he hit me so hard
and after the anger subsides
he treats me so well.

Presents and kisses
do abound that's for sure
then he tells me it's my fault,
I shouldn't argue anymore.

I forgive and I am sorry
for what I did
to make him so angry
to treat me like this.

I find familiarity
in the abuse I am given
both verbal and physical.
It is something I know well,
a past belief that is strong,
you're no good,
you're not worthy,
you deserve this living hell.

There comes a point
where I find the strength
to break this vicious cycle
of violent intent.

I stay at a house
for abused women,
it is sad.

To see all the women
learning how to be strong,
to stay away from that man
who brainwashed them to believe
that they are nothing,
they are worthless
they deserved what they got…indeed.

Run away, run away,
run as fast as you can
from that man who says he loves you
and then hits you with his hand.

You are so worthy
I tell you true,
I know this inside me
as I were such as you.

The following poem was written in the present at the same time as I wrote the above. I am a little taken aback as to all of the gaps that I have in my memory, as well as not being able to remember the timelines. I think, at this time, it is important to remind everyone that what you are reading comes from an understanding of how I perceive my memories at this point in time in my life. That being said, events and happenings are skewed by time. It is also my skewed memory that can haunt me, on a sometimes daily basis. In the second poem, *Truth*, which I wrote in the preface, it states that truth lies with the beholder. No one else can say what is true or what is false to another person as they have never had the experiences, felt the feelings, or heard the words in the manner that was provided to the teller of the story…to the holder of those feelings.

Memory

The blocks in my memory
so many I find,
I am missing entire sections,
it is hard on my mind.

My memory has failed me
of that I am sure.
Why don't I know?
Do I really care?

It does perplex me,
is it a self-survival tool
or something else entirely?
I am not a fool.

I am missing entire years,
what did I do?

It is locked in a safe
whose key I do not have,
maybe sometime in the future
it will reveal
those past experiences
that are hidden so deep
it seems surreal.

My husband and I, are living in Saskatoon, SK. I remember getting a job at Fairweather, which is a women's clothing store in Canada, doing sales. I was quite good, and they were looking to make me a manager, surprise, surprise. We were quite broke, except Al always found the money to buy expensive suits. Why The Fuck (can you feel the emotion behind this?) he needed a thousand-dollar suit to sell vacuums I have no idea. I, on the other hand, did not even have enough money to buy a winter coat. I was wearing a big sweater that I had knitted for him. One time I broke one of my shoes at the store. I did not have enough money to go and buy an extra pair of shoes.

The marriage doesn't last long, just past our one-year anniversary. He started to become violent. Both verbal and physical abuse. The last night we were together it got so bad I was screaming for someone to help me. There was a couple living downstairs in the basement. I learned after that they heard my screams and, instead of doing anything, they prayed for me. I finally got out of there wearing a dress with no shoes or coat, and I ran. It was in the middle of winter with snow on the ground. I found a phone and made my way to a friend's place. I had bruises around my neck from him trying to strangle me.

Hmm, what is it with the neck? Bruises, strangulation, noose, I am only now putting things together to make sense of what happened in order to let go. One only needs understanding to obtain compassion and empathy for something that occurred. I was never heard at a young age, never able to let my voice free. Oh what trauma can be infused at such an early age. To have release take decades to recognize and then heal. To become the me that I know I AM.

I check into a house for abused women and stay there for as long as I can. I am still working at Fairweather, my sales have gone down though. I find out that Al has been calling the house I am staying at incessantly and trying to commit suicide. The workers at the house will not allow the abusive partners to contact the residents, it's a safety thing. I was told by the workers that he was hospitalized for suicide attempts. I didn't talk to him to find out what happened.

We learn all about the cycle of abuse at the women's shelter. We get excited when a bag of donated clothes comes to the door and we all scramble down to go through what treasures were brought in. The majority of us had to run away from where we were living with our partners, with only what we could carry in one arm. It is not an easy thing to leave an abusive partner.

Sometimes we get home-made baking; once again we are all thrilled. Such simple things bring joy to those who have nothing. There are young ones and old ones, with and without children. It is a sad situation that so many women get abused. And this isn't the first time that some of them have been there. As a condition for staying there, we have to take classes that teach about the cycle of abuse. I learn a lot. The time comes close to me having to leave. I have nowhere in Saskatoon to go, I feel at a loss. I end up calling my mother and going back to Winnipeg as she has been supportive, compassionate and strong for me during this process.

Quite a few years later, I am living in St. Albert with my second husband and I see a picture in the Edmonton newspaper in the entertainment section. It had a picture of my ex-husband Al on it saying that he was the lead singer of a blues band in Edmonton. I never even knew he could sing. I had not talked to him since I left Saskatoon. It gave me a strange feeling to know that he had been living in the same town as I had, for who knows how long. In my mind, I thought, *Yeah, you left him and then he started singing the blues.* In a way that was my way of making light of what happened. I still had those feelings of inadequacy, of being wrong, of not being worthy. Oh, when will these feelings end? I have the strength inside to know better. That strength, the real me, always shows up when I am in dire need.

Below is another poem that came through as I was in the middle of writing the above. These poems jump out in the middle of my writing and I go to my other Word document and write them down. Then I read, and I cry, and I release, and I give light to the darkness. As I have paid my dues over and over again I do not want to live my life in this turmoil anymore.

Abuse II

On a cold winter's night
I say something wrong,
we get into a fight
and the damage is done.

Harsh words are said
with an attack like a viper
digging deep into the soul,
he is a wicked fighter.

Hands around neck,
I cannot breathe,
kicking and screaming.
Oh, do help me,
please!

My calls are heard
by the neighbors below,
they huddle together
and pray for my soul.

Assistance is not coming.
I find in myself
a strength so strong
I am not giving up.

I find a way out
as he goes to the bathroom;
I sneak out the front door
and run for my life.

The marriage does end,
the divorce is final.
I am amazed and in awe
of the strength that arose
to disrupt that endless circle
of abusive blows.

This poem came at the end of my writing for this day. Not more that I need to say…

Strength

The more I read
the more I cry;
the more it heals
and my heart sighs.

The poems I am writing
are not for the lighthearted,
some will see the truth within their own being
to understand they are not alone.
Others have gone through a nightmare

to find the strength
to seek for help.

To let out the demons
deep down inside
to give them love
that was once forgotten
that is the strength
that we abide.

The trauma,
the fear,
the loss,
the exhaustion
assists the strength
within
to know
we are not forgotten.

We have the power
within each of us
to change the situation
that leaves us amiss.

To know
we are not alone
that others
reside along with us
to let go of the abuse
let go of the old habits
that keep us locked
in our own living hell.

The grass is greener
on this other side
for the grass grows within us,
all we need
is to look inside.

CHAPTER 10

2017

Poetry from the Present as the Writing has Ceased for a Bit

The writing of my memoirs has come to a slow decline as I feel the need to process and heal, and allow the light to come in. However, as I do this, the poetry keeps coming sporadically over a period of a month or two. These poems are ponderings about what I was feeling and what I was going through. What I had written so far was immense. It has been the foundations of what made me who I am. How the mask got created, the deep, dark secrets, the ignorance to what was happening. It was very surreal to write. Integration of the written word to my emotional, mental, and physical body. Time needed to flow through, to come to terms, to forgive, and then to understand. For the sake of being authentic and true, I will say that I entered a couple of times of deep depression in October when all writing stopped and a true feeling of despair entered my being. Thoughts of suicide did enter my presence. The not knowing why I was here. So much pain to get through. Yelling at the universe to assist and help me as I felt hopeless. Logical thinking about how to die, creating a plan of how to get my children what little money I still had saved so they did not have to worry about it after I was gone. A lot...I mean a LOT of tears.

Here is what came out while I was going through this phase:

To See The Light

Everyone says
to see the light
will make things right.

But how can one
only see light?
For when there is light,
darkness is present.

Fear is alight
when darkness is near
so we run away
we ignore
and we leave
the darkness inside,
it is scary indeed.

For me
I believe
the darkness needs to be felt,
to be given the light
to make it alright.

So remember
we must,
to feel it fully
is right

as it allows one to see
into the light.

A passage has opened,
the fear released
as we see what happened
to put us in this place
of darkness and hatred
self-loathing and need.

It is a progress
that is slow indeed
but so worthy to go through.

To peel the layers
that were ingrained so deep,
to change that story
that you so believed.

To allow the light
to enter your soul,
to become the true you
that deserves
so much more.

I love you, sweet one,
that is so true,
you are perfect
in everything that you do.

This is the new story:
you are worthy,
you are new,

you are complete,
you are love,
you…
are simply you.

The light
that everyone seeks
is already
a part
of the wonderful being
that is called
YOU.

All The Men

All the men
that have come
and gone.

I look back and see
the good,
the bad,
the unworthy,
the worthy.

To look back
at the chances not taken
to where life could have gone.

Could I have been a much happier person
if a different man was chosen?
I think not

for my inner being
was still me.

Damaged and torn
beyond repair
not knowing that my past
was taking me there.

The decisions
that were made
were not best for me
for they came from
the past
of pure need.

The neediness came through my soul
so lost and forgotten,
I needed to be whole.

Then the time came where
I told it to stop.
I will not live life
from experiences
that taught me
so many wrong things
that told me
I was not worthy of love.

To the universe I asked
to give me help,
to stop living in the past.
I have paid my dues

I want to be me,
no more blues.

From that step forward
I focused on release,
let the demons out
set them free.

All the light
that I gave to others
I give to myself
so I could heal
to learn the lessons
and set the past free
so I can live life in harmony.

Funk

Here I sit
in a funk
not able to think,
just sad and alone.

Time to give
myself a kick in the ass.

You are better than this,
you tell yourself.

It does not help.
I talk to my friends,
they are in the same mood,

not happy,
not really sad,
just brooding.

I feel stuck
like a truck in mud
with the wheels not turning,
just heavy and laden.

I can't stay like this,
It's driving me mad.
I think a walk will do
to open me up,
take some fresh air
deep into my lungs.

Give myself the will
to become one.

A split personality,
the fear behind the mask
is ruling my life
in the here and now.

Smoke too much,
eat bad food,
nothing is helping,
is it time to rule?

Others have found love,
I have not,
am I looking too hard,
is my mask not in place?

Is this the life
I am meant to live,
alone and lonely
with no one to love?

OK time to go
for a very fast stroll,
power-walk away
the lost little soul.

Exercise it will be
as I can't sit here anymore,
I need to move on
to find my happy place,
to get to the authentic soul.

Then home I will come
to write up a storm
my book, I am told,
that will help everyone.

Darkness

Hello darkness, my old friend,
you are here with me again,
you hold my hand
like you belong
to take me into
my deepest fears,
to spread the light
and allow the tears.

To take the mask off
and be strong
for you are alive
and you are worth
all the love that
was torn
from long ago
maybe since you were born.

The past it haunts
it creates such fear,
flight or fight
is always near.

It takes such warmth,
a loving embrace,
a show of heart,
to finally replace
the darkness that does reside
deep down inside.

Become aware of when it rises
to make the change
so it subsides
to give you love
when you need it most.

Knowing the love you have inside,
this powerful force will help you win
the light that has been so very dim.

To live and laugh and breathe with joy
it can be done,
it's a part of you.

So stay aware and replace the dark
with the light and love
from your heart
to become the one
that you have dreamed
to rescue you
so you no longer bleed.

Mask

Take off the mask
that your ego has worn
to hide your fears
of which you were sworn.

Those past beliefs,
alone and afraid,
for if someone sees
they will run away scared.

Is this the you
who you truly are
for sure not real
alone in the dark?

The mask will not hold,
the past will appear
when you least expect it
jumping out clear.

Feel the past
in all its glory,

it is holding you back,
tell your real story.
Vocalize
what you thought was bad
for to give it the light.
is to reduce the past.

The past of
fear,
self-loathing
and hate.

The past
so false
it needs to abate.

The true you
is awaiting inside
to be let free,
awake in delight.

The following poem was written for my dear Brendan, a part of my soul, a part of my being, a twin flame that still resides in the world that is paper and money and drugs and alcohol and work. All the things that keep one numb, not able to move. When Brendan first arrived to Playa del Carmen, we kept bumping into each other for the first three weeks as we have a lot of friends in common. I kept having this feeling that I needed to talk to him. When we finally did get a chance to talk, it was like being at home. Comfort abounded and aided the voice to be heard. Brendan will always have a special place in my heart. No matter where he goes or what he does, he will always be a part of me. He was the catalyst that started my writing, and forever I will feel blessed to have met him.

To Love Someone

To love someone
is truly a blessed event,
but when that someone is far
distant in time,
distant in memory,
distant in geography,
does that love fade?

Love changes
and grows
and becomes
something different.

A flame so bright
it burns so fast
you feel
from the deepest part of your soul
from your entire being
it is wild,
it is wonderful,
it is amazingly surreal!

To end so fast
as fast as it started
the distance is far,
life takes over,
the memory fades
into the night.

But the heart still remembers
the love that was there,
the longing subsides
and what remains
is a warm glow inside.

No needing,
no wanting,
no thoughtful despair
as a blessing was given
when you entered
my lair.

I think of you often,
warm, loving embrace
that binds us together
in that special place.

A place without walls,
no boundaries,
no fears,
a place that is all-encompassing,
the universe…
It appears.

I wish you well
in all that you do,
you are a special soul
connected to me
as me to you.

Memories

To write of your memories
the past hurts and pains
puts one in a place
of dreadful disdain.

Oh, why me?
What happened was wrong,
the poor little girl
and the resulting harm.

Many years have passed,
I look back and see
the cause and effect
that beheld me.

I sit here in awe
seeing the strength,
the will,
the courage
that resided deep in me.

To live through life
as a damaged being
but not willing to give up,
to keep going
and going.

The heartache and pain,
the not knowing why,
shall I try to end it again?
No

No
No
Not I!

I feel truly blessed
to be where I am,
to be who is me
to live and be strong.

My heart is now mending,
the memories are stories,
the blessings are many.
I am to succeed,
to finish my life,
to help those in need.

Touch Me

Touch me,
feel me,
penetrate my soul,
make me yours.
I have no where else to go.

Open me up
like a ripe, juicy fruit,
touch me like no other.
Oh, it feels so good.

Deep inside there is a blessing to behold,
treat it with care

as there is only one,
do not destroy
for it cannot be undone.

I take you inside,
deep into my being,
to allow you to feel
what keeps me real.

Honor the me
of who I know I am
and I will treat you so well,
you will begin to understand

The bounty I hold
inside my being,
waiting for the right person
to allow the feeling.

The feeling of love,
compassion
and joy
to set me free,
allow me
to be me.

No more hiding
in dark corners,
suspect in waiting
not trusting anyone.

Set me free to fly
like a beautiful butterfly,

give me wings
to sail on the wind.

Open me up
and take me with ease,
all it takes
is understanding,
compassion,
love,
empathy,
and a true being
to be true to me.

I wrote the poem below while on a trip to Cabo with my brother, his wife, and another couple. We had an ocean front room that looked onto the waves crashing into the rocks.

Paradise

Sitting in paradise
looking at the ocean,
waves come in tumbling,
hitting the rocks
with wild emotion.

No time to be sad,
peaceful feeling at its best,
what a life.
Oh my,
I am so blessed.

Drink in hand,
ocean liner by the pier,

infinity pool
is oh so near.

Dark blue sparkling water,
my mind is clear,
in my heart
there is no trouble,
it's all about
lack of fear.

To come to a place
of bliss
after my life
was so amiss.

I no longer wonder
as my head is no longer
taking control of
me,
myself
and I.

It is time
to
feel fine.

Everything I went through
now is just a story
that I can tell
without
fear,
without fright,

without it taking control
of my here and now.

I am in a place of bliss,
true contentment at its best.
I am so thankful
for everything that happened
to bring me
to the here,
to the now,
to this place of
happiness
that I know
right now.

Dragon Fly

A dragonfly
I found
alone in my room,
trapped behind the screen
waiting for me.

To give me a message
that change is near.

Everything that has passed
is true and clear,
it made me who I am,
gave me the lessons
that needed to be learned

To trust in myself,
my strength,
my true being.

The time is now.

To forgive those
that need to be forgiven.

To love those
that need to be loved.

To hear those
that need to be heard.

To feel
fully and truly.

Bliss is what I feel,
bliss is my reward
for living a life
from the bottom of my soul.

Time

Time takes its toll
as everyone knows,
we all grow old
before our time
or so it seems.

Fleeting moments
is all that is there;

the memories past,
those that are remembered
seem lost in time
along the way.

What stays near and dear
are the emotions that were felt
along the path
we call life.

But why, oh why
are feelings that haunt us
the bad memories
that keep us held
in the prison
called our mind?

Stop I say,
I do not want to be here
in the past that was so
horrendous with shame.

They hold on tight,
the fears and the tears,
for to let them go
they must be felt.

They have been around
so many, many years,
they fight to stay
to maintain control.

So try I do
to give what is needed,
to allow, to feel fully
and release them to the flame.

But, lo and behold,
another is lurking
to take the place
of that which was let free.

What a wicked web
this thing we call life,
these are lessons to be learned
all this hurt and strife.

Yes, I read,
you need to believe,
it is your soul seeking understanding
in order to move on.

For if your life was easy
what would you learn,
what strength would you have?
You would have none.

It is with this belief
I allow my soul
to learn the lessons I am learning,
to forgive,
better yet
to understand.

So here I sit
with tears a streaming
with so many memories
waiting their turn.

A life truly lived
is lived through experience,
I now re-live those experiences
so I can become
the me that is there,
the strength that I see,
the strength that is me,
which pulled me along.

Along through the tough times
it didn't let me give up.
As I sit here
I see the past that once hurt
has given me knowledge
that I do deserve

Deserve a life with compassion,
empathy and understanding,
for how can I be these things
without knowing the other world?

CHAPTER 11

July 1985 to March 1988

Back Again to Winnipeg

When I left my husband Al, I moved back to my mom's house. I was able to get a transfer to a Fairweather store in Winnipeg as my manager felt bad for me and wanted to help. I brought my dog with me, and my mom hated the dog, because it wasn't fully trained and was peeing in the house while I was at work, so she told me I had to leave. Here I am, after leaving an abusive husband, and having spent the last couple of months in a house for abused women, and yet getting the dog out of her house was more important than helping me. Yet again, I am displaced. I went to live downtown with a girl I worked with at Fairweather and her boyfriend, Timothy. Timothy was tall and handsome, with a charismatic charm. We got along really well; he was smart and funny and made me feel good. I do have wonderful memories of him. It makes me smile to think of those times as I was getting some well-deserved attention that I felt came from the heart.

I quit my job at Fairweather as I had outgrown it, and I got a job at the *Brick*. The *Brick* was a furniture chain from Alberta, and the first store in Manitoba was opening in Winnipeg. It was a cutthroat sales job where the person with the lowest sales got fired each month. Not a healthy environment. I eventually moved out of Tim's place and stayed with his dad for a bit. I am still unsettled in my heart and in my mind, not knowing what to do. The *Brick* is really not resonating with me. My mom went up north to visit my brother who was living and working in Inuvik, NT. When she came back, she told me there were lots of opportunities for jobs up there. I take the leap and buy a return ticket to Inuvik, with the plan of staying for a week or two.

And the poetry comes out again…

Home

An abused soul
looking for a home,
lost in mind,
no place in sight.

Move I must
for the grass is
greener
on the other side.

But the other side
is never in reach.

Nothing works out,
again I must leave.

On and on I go,
looking for
something.

What?
Even I do not know.

CHAPTER 12

July 1988

Move to Inuvik, NT

I go up to Inuvik and stay with my brother and his girlfriend, Karen, for a couple of weeks. I go to the local bar, *The Zoo*; I meet people. I decide not to return to Winnipeg as I felt there was nothing left for me there. I end up staying in Inuvik for just over nine years.

Inuvik, NT is a small town in Canada of just over 3,000 people, and is located about 100 km (60 mi) from the Arctic Ocean and 200 km (120 mi) north of the Arctic Circle. There is an average of thirty days of twenty-four hour darkness in the winter, and an average of fifty-six days of twenty-four hour sunlight in the summer. There is only one gravel road, the Dempster Highway, that runs 671 km (417 mi) from the Klondike Highway near Dawson City, Yukon to Inuvik. This road has two river crossings that get shut down twice a year, once in the spring and once in the fall. This is due to the rivers freezing up (late October to mid December) to create an ice bridge. And again (mid May to mid June) to thaw out and allow ferries to transport vehicles. During these times the only way to get anything in or out of the town is by airplane.

My brother was a pilot and my dad was an airplane mechanic, and both worked for Aklak Air, a local airline servicing the north.

Just before I went to my visit my brother, my dad decided that he needed to quit his job and leave Inuvik. He left shortly before I got there. He knew I was coming and we hadn't seen each other in years. Not important enough to stay a few days to see me I guess. It figures. Why should I care? It was a habitual thing for my dad to get up and leave. He was never there for me even if I was around. He has become a sperm donor, someone who fucked my mother. So, I ask myself, why does it still hurt?

My brother helped me get an apartment as well as a job at Aklak Air. I was a clerk and I knew nothing about computers. One of the first things they had me doing was formatting the old floppy disks. Not a hard job, format a: except I made a mistake and formatted c: then the shit hit the fan…oops. I may have been hung over…oh well. It was hard to find good people to work in the north, so they took the chance and kept me on.

Not long after I decided to stay in Inuvik, Karen, my brother's girlfriend, was walking up the large flight of stairs to her apartment and she had an asthma attack. It was pretty bad. She was hospitalized and later medivacked out, flown out of Inuvik to a hospital in Edmonton. She had some brain damage and the Inuvik Hospital was not equipped to help her. My brother stayed with her and helped her through her recovery, leaving Inuvik and leaving me. It was OK, I understood; life goes on and I have always been alone.

The place to go partying was a local bar called *The Zoo.* I started dating the bar manager, Jeff. "Why?" you may ask. But of course, the answer is he paid attention to me, he was also a lot of fun and we got along well. It was a relationship with alcohol and drugs and sex. I did fall in love—or what I thought was love then. It ended bitterly with me finding him in one of the hotel rooms in bed with another girl. That was the end of the relationship. I ended up having breakup sex with him a while after. It was October 1989.

Just before, I decided to go and see a doctor, to inform them of what I had learned at age of fifteen, that I may not be able to get pregnant. I truly believed it to be the case as I was not on any type of birth control pill and, so far, had not gotten pregnant. Not that I wanted to get pregnant, I just wanted to know the truth. I went and had a laparoscopy. The results, one Fallopian tube was completely damaged with scar tissue. No chance of an egg coming from that one. The other tube was badly scarred. The doctor said that the chances of getting pregnant were very, very slim. OK, I now know the truth. Or so I thought. The breakup sex with Jeff, not protected, ended up with me getting pregnant. I think what happened was that the scope, from the laparoscopy, cleared a path in the one Fallopian tube that was wide enough for an egg to drop down and get fertilized. In any case, I am now twenty-four, single, and pregnant.

To Give Birth

What once could be
was told not so,
this truth to me
was not a harsh blow.

To give birth
was not a priority
for I did not know
how to be.

The longing need
to give birth to another
was lost in life,
I did not bother.

A test to see
if it was true
led me to believe
I would not conceive.

Oh, but life has a way
of leading you astray
of saying, "Oh, this is what you think,
ha, ha, ha…not today."

It is time again
to turn you upside down,
another lesson
for you to learn.

Can you leave your past
to give birth
to a new life
in this world?

Let go of the pain
once held so deep
to not let it in
to set this one free.

After I found Jeff in bed with this girl, I talked to my boss at Aklak Air as I had nowhere to live. At that time, I was living with Jeff. My boss set me up in a house with two other employees of Aklak Air. Kevin and Paul. Kevin is a year or two younger than me, he is tall and handsome and kind and caring and funny. We start a relationship. It is only for us, not for anyone to know. We laugh, and we giggle, and we talk. He is wonderful. I am not sure why it didn't go any further. Maybe it had something to do with me getting pregnant. I found out many years later that Kevin always had a thing for me and wanted to try to start something after he got back from school down south. But I was in a relationship with my soon to be husband Rob, and nothing happened.

CHAPTER 13

June 11, 1990

Gave Birth to Michael

I never wanted children. I was never the maternal type. It was not an inherent characteristic. It never really bothered me when I found out I could probably never have children. When I got pregnant, there was no thought in my mind of having an abortion or giving him up for adoption. Jeff was nowhere to be seen or heard so I knew I would be doing this alone. Jeff actually left town before I had the baby. I never got any type of support, financially, physically or emotionally, from him. I found an apartment that would subsidize my rent as I could not afford full rent by myself. Being pregnant is not something that bodes well for me. I become huge. So huge, in fact, that my brother does not recognize me when he comes to see me just before I give birth and starts calling me Aunt Jemima. Not something that a nine-month-pregnant woman wants to hear. Sigh...

When I give birth to my son, there are many people present. In the hospital room there were three people, Ashley and two friends. There were several people waiting outside as well, my mother included. I gave birth to a beautiful, healthy boy.

I learned a lot being a mother. It wasn't easy doing it all alone.

But I did persevere. The maternal instincts kicked in and, all of a sudden, I could hold and feed and take care of a baby. I remember Michael crying all throughout the night with me crying and rocking him and not knowing what to do. At times, it was scary, and I felt utterly out of control. My mother was always there on the other side of the phone helping and supporting me.

During this period, I could only get three months for paid maternity leave through Unemployment Insurance. Back to work I go with a three-month-old baby at the baby sitter's. I remember her being a very nice old Inuit lady. I would pick him up after work and he would be nice and clean and smelling like baby powder. I was sad that I could not spend more time with him. About a year after his birth, I met a man, his name was Rob. He had seen me around town. I was told he had a crush on me and he wanted to know who I was. Inuvik, being a small town, has a lot of single women who immediately go after men as soon as they arrive. I have never been able to do that. To go after a man. They had always gone after me. I think it was because I was too scared and afraid of what may happen. Also, a big factor was because I did not know how to talk, did not know what to say. I never learned the gift of the gab. Always silent and alone, an introvert at heart.

In any case, Rob contacted me and made the first moves. Then we moved in together and we got married just over a year later.

CHAPTER 14

June 19, 1993

Married Rob

Rob was handsome and funny and intelligent. We had fun together. He took to Michael right away and officially adopted him. Rob is Michael's true father in every sense of the word. For this, I will always love and appreciate him. At this time, life had calmed down for me. I had a loving husband, a baby boy, a good job, and no need to worry about money. It was perfect. Well, almost perfect, as I had demons inside me, demons of past events and beliefs that were ingrained into my being, things that I had pushed down and ignored. Why, oh why do the demons decide to come out when I am happy, when I should be happy? As it was, in a normal sober state of life I am good. When I drink and someone says something to trigger me is when all the hurt comes out. The mind and the mask get pushed aside and my pain shows its ugly head. I had incidents of this in the past. But most of the past relationships were not healthy ones so I figured I had a right to get angry, a right to yell and scream. For the most part I think I was right to let the anger come out. However, when it came out, it was full force. It was all the hurt and the pain and the not understanding. I was horrible, I knew the right words to say to have the most devastating impact. I had learned my lessons well as a youngster. This, I knew, was not me. This was someone else. I had no idea where it was coming from. I became the verbal abuser during these times of anger. It was not that I was angry all the time. For most of the relationship it was fine.

Part of me needed to communicate, needed to talk, needed to be heard, especially when I was feeling down. I had lost my voice a long time ago, but I still needed to get things out. One should be able to talk, to open up, and to be vulnerable with the person who says they love you. I had a desire to take off my mask. I was also terribly afraid. So, rather than say things outright, I would talk circles around the issue hoping that the other person would understand, would get what I meant. I look back and can see, can feel, how hard I tried. But every time I tried and did not get understood, it put a brick up in the wall. And you see, that wall got built ever so high over the years adding layers to the onion of past beliefs, past trauma.

In any case, Rob and I got married in Inuvik. Of course, my father was not there. I did not even bother to invite him. It was a beautiful ceremony. A few months later, we went on our honeymoon to Florida. We had decided that we would try to have a baby. Since Michael was born I had been using birth control pills. I went off the pills for the honeymoon. In Florida, we were staying at a condo of a friend of Rob's. The room had two single beds, which we pushed together. That was the night when my daughter, Tandia, was conceived.

CHAPTER 15

July 1, 1994

Gave Birth to Tandia

July 1,1994, I am standing outside Inuvik Regional Hospital and my mother and son are at my side. The black flies are out biting us, as it is that time of year. The Canada Day Parade is getting ready to start. I am having contractions because I was induced that morning. It seems that my little bundle of joy likes where she is and doesn't want to come out. The parade goes by and I go back into the hospital to walk the halls in the hope of moving things along faster. Later that afternoon, the contractions come stronger and I get ready to go to the labor room. Rob, my husband, is with me. It is supper time. I know this because no one told the kitchen that I was in labor, so they brought my supper to the labor room. Rob was there to hold my hand during a contraction, then went to eat my supper in between. I was not pleased as I was in pain and could not eat. Now I can look back and laugh. A beautiful baby girl was born that day.

We did not find out what the sex of the baby was when I was pregnant so we picked a boy's and a girl's name. Rob is very much into my heritage. My parents were born in South Africa; however, both are a mixture of nationalities, German, British, Polynesian, Filipino, Zulu and a few more I cannot remember. In any case, Rob wants to have a name that reflects my heritage; me, not so much as I really have no idea what my heritage is. I get frustrated and say, "OK, we can name her after one of my relatives from South Africa. Here are their names: Doreen, Lydia, Julia. Which one of the South African names do you want to use?" He was not amused. I thought it was funny. Rob had read this book, *The Power of One* by Bryce Courtney. He gave it to me to read early in the relationship and I really liked it. The sequel to the book was called *Tandia* and it was about this strong, powerfully beautiful girl who grew up in devastation and survived. I loved the book and this girl's story. I felt emotionally attached to her story and how she survived. I suggested naming our daughter Tandia. And so it was that Tandia Mercedes Feagan came into the world.

Postpartum Depression

What a beautiful sight
the first time I saw you,
a bundle of joy
entering into this world.

All my hopes and dreams
wrapped up into one,
a precious little girl
to behold and to love

Treasure and protect;
that was my job.

But, oh, those past memories,
why can't you leave me alone?

The rush of emotions
took hold once again.

As I hold my dear daughter
tears rush from my eyes,
how could anyone hurt
such a small little life?

I was given up,
a token to be used,
at the age of nine
allowed to be abused.

How could one
give birth to someone
and then so fleetingly
allow damage to be done?

Postpartum depression
set in right away,
the poor lonely me
crying out in pain.

I am now a mother
of a beautiful girl,
how could someone
intentionally hurt me
so long ago?

My pain was deep
as it was never released
and came rushing in freely
to take me to a place

of lonely and sad,
not worthy and more.

I had no control
of the anguish I felt,
it was too close to home,
a mother and daughter,
oh God, how it hurt.

I sit there alone
with my daughter in her crib
so desperately grieving
the loss of my soul.

The pills on the table
count them one more time
in the tears that rush down.
I can't live anymore.

My heart is crushed,
the pain too severe.
I can't do this anymore,
I need to end this
I fear.

As the tears subside
I look over at my babe,
the strength comes in slowly
like a silent whisper.

I know you are hurting,
my love, that is me,

but you must go on living
in the future you will see.

The world needs you here,
you may not feel it now,
put away those pills,
pick up that babe that you love.

Hold her so tight,
feel her purity,
that pure, innocent light,
grab hold of it, please.

Wipe away those tears
it is not time for you to pass.

I step into a deep-seated postpartum depression. You see, I have pushed down all of the emotions and traumas from my past and have never dealt with them. Having a beautiful baby girl triggered all the pain that I had pushed down and it erupted like a volcano. How could anyone do harm to such an innocent being? Not just any innocent being but one they carried for nine months and gave birth to. How? How? How? The volcano explodes, and I am desperately depressed. I cry all the time. I cry for the little girl that was me. I cry for what I went through. I cry for not being good enough to be loved. I cry, I cry, and I cry.

This has to stop, I seek help. I go to this group for people struggling with depression. We have to dig deep and tell our stories. *I have never told my story...I can't...It's horrendous...People will look at me differently. I will be looked down upon. I will be shamed; people will think it is my fault. My mask will need to come down.* I had hit bottom, so the story came out. Slowly, my mouth moved, then my voice whispered. It told of the abuse and the anguish of that nine-year-old girl. It got its first wisp of air, the first telling of what happened.

The leader of the group said that it was best if we could find someone to support us outside of the group, someone whom we could tell the story to so that they could love and support us during this difficult time. I sat down that night on one side of the couch. Rob was on the other side of the couch. I haltingly told pieces of my story. I explained why I was telling him. I told him I needed help. I told him I needed support. I told him it was not pretty. I told him that it may take a while for the story to come out as my voice was lost so long ago. He sat there and listened and did not move. I am not sure if he said anything, but I felt him moving away from me. No compassion, no empathy, nothing. Here I sit, letting down my mask to the person who says he loves me. To get no reaction. I am alone again, a boulder being placed on the wall of our relationship to push us even further apart. This, I think, was the beginning of the end. It was many years later that Rob talked to me and said that he could not be there for me when I was telling my story or going through depression as it triggered a past trauma in his life, it brought up his own emotions that he could not deal with. I, once again, am devastated.

I am alone again with my past haunting me. I am suicidal, I don't want to be here anymore. What I learned in my past is strong again. *You are not worthy, no one loves you, you are bad, you are wrong, it is your fault.* I don't know how to handle it, I don't know how to cope.

We have a fight one morning, Rob wants to take Michael to another town to play hockey. I am asking him to stay, I am crying, I am telling him that I need him. He packs up and leaves with Michael. I am devastated. I am left alone with the tornado of past hurts wreaking havoc within my being. I decide I cannot do this anymore. I go and find every pill that I have. I put them all on the table. I put Tandia in her playpen beside me. I cry, and I look at the pills and I count them. I wonder if it is enough. I can't take them until I know Rob is on his way home because I don't want Tandia to be by herself for too long. She is just a baby. I count, and I wait, and I cry. I cry until I am so tired I put my head on the table and pass out. I wake to Tandia crying. I pick her up and I realize that I cannot do this. She has become my strength to live. I put away the pills and I look after her. My heart is still torn, the pain still resides deep inside me. The strength has found me again, it tells me to keep on going. It is not my time.

I talk to the doctor and he puts me on antidepressants. They help a bit. They put a fog in my brain so that the pain from the memories subsides. It is like covering a bleeding wound with a piece of whispery gauze. Just enough to stop the blood from spurting but nothing to help the wound heal.

I continue with life in a haze.

CHAPTER 16

1995

Life in Inuvik

I am now thirty, and there is a couple that we are friends with, Linda and Keith. I like both of them and Linda and I become friends. Over some drinks at their place Linda and I have a conversation. I know that the words need to come out. They are lying in wait to be heard and let free. I open up to Linda and talk about what happened and my depression. I take the mask off; I need to let it out, I need to tell my story and Linda gives me a safe space in order to be able to do this. I find out that she had gone through a similar experience with her brothers. This was my first understanding that I was not alone in what I went through. There are others. It gave me a breath of hope to know that others have gone through traumatic events in their life and are still here and are surviving with it. I received love and compassion and empathy and a mostly non-judgmental ear to talk to, something that I have never gotten before other than with counselors who are paid to listen.

My work is going well. History repeats itself and, once again, I am bored at my job. At Aklak Air I started as a clerk and ended up as acting CFO. For the Inuvik Regional Health Board (IRHB) I started as a payroll clerk, then payroll manager, and then acting

CFO. My mind is sharp. I helped select and implement the new payroll software at the IRHB. I became extremely proficient with the software and spent lots of time on the phone with the developers helping them make it better. My logical mind loves this challenge albeit I, once again, get bored and decide to start my own business consulting with other health boards in the NT, helping them with their payroll.

CHAPTER 17

June 1996 to March 1997

Self-Employed

I am excited, I have my own business and I am getting paid a lot of money. I travel over to Iqaluit to do some consulting. It was a bit of a mess over there and I ended up staying for a month or so. I was missing my children though. When I got back to Inuvik, I got a call from Ormed, the company whose software I had helped implement for IRHB. They were looking for someone to work for them down in Edmonton. Rob and I decided that it was a good time to move down south in order to give the kids access to more things. Michael was turning out to be a great little hockey player and there was more access for him to develop down in Alberta.

It was a big decision, to pack up our life and move. About a year before, we had sold our big house and now were living in a smaller row house. We had a lot of friends and had made a life for ourselves. Rob would have to quit his job and find a new job down south. I had to take a drastic cut in pay. I had been living in Inuvik now for just over nine years. It seemed like a lifetime, but life moves on and so must we. This had been the most stable I had been in a long time. I had no second thoughts about packing up and moving. So move we did.

CHAPTER 18

March 1997 to August 1999

Moved to St. Albert, AB

We decided that we did not want to move to a big city. We had heard a lot of good things about St. Albert as it was right beside Edmonton and was a smaller, family-oriented city with lots of things for the kids to do. We had gotten used to living in a small town and a big city was a little unnerving.

Working for Ormed was exhilarating and mind expanding. I was doing everything related to the payroll software, other than actually writing the code. I was sales, implementation, support, product manager and project manager. It was a great place to work. Lots of very smart people, most of them with accounting designations, and I was given the ability to manage myself. Within a month of me getting there they sent me to a small town outside of Toronto to demonstrate the software. I was scared as I had only driven our little truck in Inuvik for the last nine years. Never once had I driven in a city in that entire time. Now I am heading off by myself and tackling the six-lane highways of Toronto. This, for me, was scary and nerve-wracking, I hated it. Obviously, I survived, and I thrived in the fast-paced atmosphere of work.

There are little things that you forget about when living in a small town, one of those things is to recognize landmarks when driving to a place in order to find your way back out. On my first trip to a small town just outside Toronto, I was heading to the hospital and I thought, *Wow this is awesome; all I had to do was follow the H signs.* I was very nervous about this first meeting so my mind was preoccupied. Once I was done with the meeting, I got out to the car, sat down and then realized that I had no idea how to get back to the highway. OMG, I shuffled my way back to the reception to meekly ask for directions on how to get back. This was the first and last time that I forgot to look for landmarks.

Ormed sold software to hospitals and health boards all over Canada. My travel schedule was crazy, spending two to three weeks a month on the road. I excelled. My time at home was always busy with the kids, making Halloween costumes, cooking, cleaning and running around. Rob was having a hard time finding a job. He spent a lot of time with the kids doing things with them.

Our relationship was never really the same after my postpartum depression. It didn't help that I spent long periods away from home. I worked my ass off. In the two years I worked for Ormed I went from making $30,000 a year to $80,000 a year and had won the Employee of the Year award two years in a row. Yes, me, with a Grade 12 GED and no other schooling. All of the other employees had some kind of accounting designation.

However, I burned myself out and could not find the energy to work there anymore. They were not happy to see me go, but it was time. It had been two years…sigh. I contracted myself out to write manuals for them. This was a nice income while looking for my next career move.

During the last year of working at Ormed I was training someone to assist me. My trainee was a man and we got to know each other quite well as we spent a lot of time together. With my relationship not doing great and the travel on the road, I ended up having an affair. He was also married with a child. It was not the best decision of my life and I came to realize after a month or so that it could not keep going on. I decided to end it. When I made this decision, I was relieved. I thought that I should give it a good try with Rob and my behavior changed.

I remember happily cooking in the kitchen and feeling good about the decisions that I was making. I got a call a bit earlier, and it was the person who I had the affair with saying that he did not want it to end. I told him it was 100% over. There I am, high on life and feeling good about moving forward with my relationship with my husband. All of a sudden, Rob calls me into the bedroom and tells me that he had tapped the phone and had a tape of the conversation I just had. It devastated me. What just happened? What did I do? Rob was very upset. I was very upset. Everything had just come tumbling down in rubbles beneath my feet.

About a year earlier we, as a family, went to Mazatlán, Mexico for a vacation. In Mexico, at that time, you could buy antibiotics without a prescription. A few years back, when I was living in Inuvik, I had to take antibiotics and I was prescribed a sulfa drug. A couple of hours after I took the medication I blew up like a balloon, not able to move, falling in and out of consciousness. I called Rob for help. He was too busy and never came until his work was finished. There I am again, alone and sick and not able to do anything and not having anyone there. When Rob got home, I made him take me to the hospital. They took one look at me, took me into emergency and started doing tests right away. They thought it could be meningitis, so they gave me a spinal tap. In the end, it ended up being a very bad allergic reaction to the sulfa medication. This experience put another brick in the wall of my relationship with my husband.

Here I am in Mexico, in a relationship that has a lot of bricks in the wall. Depression is not readily within my everyday existence, but I still do think about it every once in a while. I go into the pharmacy and buy a few boxes of sulfa medication. Just in case. It is like a safety net. I know I have it around and it is there. It makes me feel better. I kept it with me and never thought of using it—until Rob confronted me with the tape of the conversation that I had. As I said, I was devastated, not for being caught but for causing so much hurt to someone else. I was not thinking straight, my body had adrenaline coursing through it. I immediately went into a severe state of depression. I found the pills and took them. Rob came into the room and asked me what I had done. I wouldn't tell him. Then he found the boxes. I am not really sure how I got to the hospital. I remember them pumping me full of something and having to throw up this thick, black liquid continuously. They got to me in time for it not to be fatal. A girlfriend picked me up, Rob must have called her, and I went to a hotel. I laid there on the bed, I don't know how many days, it could have been two or five or seven, my memory is gone.

Rob and I started talking. I opened up and became vulnerable. I told him of the wall and everything that went into building it up. He told me how he felt. We still loved each other. We decided to give it another try. We decided to have a second marriage ceremony. To show our commitment to each other.

Suicide

Oh, how bitter the pill is
when you swallow.

Oh, how bitter the emotions are
when you decide to end it.

How hard
is your life?

How painful
are your memories?

How much hurt
do you feel?

How hopeless
does it seem?

To make the decision
to end your life.

Does the thought of others
enter your mind?

Of course it does,
it will do them no harm.

You are helping them
such as you are helping you.

For what person wants to be
with someone like you?

I cry many tears
for those who have thought

That their life is not worth living
for I have been there with them

In the same space and time.

I love you, my dear ones,
so much hurt and sorrow you feel.

Let me tell you this much,
you are worthy as you are.

This is but a road bump
in the highway of your life.

A time to take a pause
and feel what has built up.

Heal the old hurts,
kiss goodbye all the pain.

Find the one deserving
of all the love you have.

For you know more than any
you have love to give.

Give it to yourself,
hug yourself as one.

Love your inner being
so that this may pass.

There is a reason for you to be here,
you have not gotten there yet.

You need to stay alive
to find your purpose in this life.

This is a chance to let go
of what it is that hurts you so.

Breathe deep into your soul,
allow the white light to enter and heal.

Breathe out with all you have,
expel all that needs to let go.

On top of it all, remember
I love you,
I do.
I know
from the bottom of my heart
you are a dear soul.

…From me … to me … for me…

CHAPTER 19

November 11, 2017

An Interlude into the Here and Now

An interlude into the presence of my here and now, November 11, 2017, just past 11:11 in the morning. I just finished listening to an online meditation for 11:11. These are magical numbers for me. I will tell the complete story of 11:11 later on in the book. But understand that this number has been paramount in my spiritual journey. It awoke me to the higher power and understanding of the I AM presence of me. As I sit here, floating in the universal energy of love, compassion, empathy and more...the message that I have for you...You are in the right place at the right time. Please, my dear beings, understand that the lessons you have learned, are learning and will continue to learn are for the highest good of yourself. Acknowledge this and seek understanding, and you will enter into the light of knowing we are all one. I love you...all of you...each and every single bit of energy floating around that makes you...you. For I am you, intertwined with your energy particles. A piece of you. I see you, I feel you, I hear you. We are all of us. With light, love and blessings, Carla.

CHAPTER 20

Fall 1998

Help Mom Pack Up in Winnipeg

My mother had decided to move to Alberta to live closer to me and my two brothers. She was packing up her house and having a hard time of it. I decided to fly down and help her as she had been living in that house for twenty-six years, and there were lots of things that needed to be parted with. I flew down and was there helping her for a few days when my sister-in-law, Ashley's wife, decided to come for a visit with the new baby. My mother was very excited to have her new grandson at her house and she wanted to show him off. She invited my Aunty Ruth and my Uncle Rex over to the house to visit and see him. This was four years after my daughter was born. Four years after I went into extreme postpartum depression. Four years after I found out the truth that my mother had already known, that Uncle Rex abused little girls and that my mother gave me up to him.

My mother, knowing what I went through, not just when I was nine but also the traumatic postpartum depression that happened after that, decided that it was more important to show off her new grandson than to have any compassion or empathy for me, for what happened to me, for what she allowed to happen to me. To even know that she talked to them, to him, invited them over...OMG, I went into a tailspin. I couldn't breathe, I couldn't be there; my mind was spiraling into a depth of depression, of unworthiness, of confusion, of heartache, of pain. I left the house before they got there.

I went to a bar, I sat there, and I drank, and I cried, and I had no idea what to do. I was alone, yet again, alone in my misery with all the postpartum depression flying back to revisit me. *How unworthy I am. Fuck, Fuck, Fuck.* Thoughts of suicide come racing back to me. *Why should I live when the one who made me thinks so little of me?* I am a mess. Everyone is staring at me. I order another drink. I chug it down. Another drink and another and another. I cry myself out and realize that I cannot sit here all night. I have nowhere to go. I am lost. My sister-in-law is calling me on my phone. For the longest time I do not answer. When I finally do, she asks where I am and then comes and meets me. I tell her what is going on and she says that my aunt and uncle have left the house. She takes me back there.

I get back to the house and go downstairs. While the thoughts of suicide are there, there is also a strength. I need help, I need to talk, and I feel that my sister-in-law is not the one that I can talk to. I call the suicide hotline and speak to someone there. They calm me down and I fall asleep on the floor. I am not aware, I do not remember what happened the next day. I am pretty sure that I just left. But I cannot say for sure. The damage was done. Actually, the damage was done years before; this was just an affirmation of how little my mother cared about me. An affirmation of the belief system that was instilled into me. However, I have moved on. I have grown, I have changed. I reached out for help. I knew it was not my fault. I could see clearer now that the little regard that my mother had for me was not mine. I would not accept it. That was her problem. I was strong. I had two children who needed me. I survived everything that was thrown at me. I have learned coping mechanisms. I have started to release. I AM worthy. Fuck Her.

CHAPTER 21

August 1999 to December 2001

Honors Degree in Computer Systems Technology

I was extremely burned out after quitting my job and it was nice working from home. At the end of the contract with Ormed I started looking for work again. While my resume had a lot of really good work experience, what it didn't have was education. Knowing how HR departments work I knew that my resume was being discarded without even being looked at as I had a Grade 12 GED with no other education. A lot of the jobs that I was looking for required degrees. I wasn't going to let that stop me. I started talking to HR departments asking what was missing on my resume. They agreed that it was the education. Then I asked them what type of education would they like to see on a resume. I did not want to go to university for four years or get an accounting designation, which takes five years.

I found out that there was a college that had a great two-year degree in computer systems technology. It was highly recognized in the industry within Edmonton, so I decided to go back to school for two years in order to get that education on my resume. Lo and behold, I could not start the course right away as they had prerequisites; Grade 12 Math and English, which I did not have. I only had a Grade 12 equivalency. They would not look at my work history to see if I could be exempted from those prerequisites. I was a bit disgruntled. Off I go, back to school to upgrade math, when I had been acting CFO of a hospital and an airline, and English, when I had been corresponding with executive officers of hospitals all over Canada. Sigh. *Well, I must do what I must do.* I excelled in school for the next two and a half years and I graduated with honors. My logical mind, so it seems, loved the challenge of writing code and creating programs.

After graduating, I found work rather quickly. The job I got was working for a company called Bellamy Software. They created financial accounting systems for businesses, including payroll software. I was there to replace one of their employees who was taking a hiatus to Australia for a year.

About a month or two after I started with Bellamy, I got a call from Carl. He worked for a company called Vision Pay. Vision Pay developed payroll and HR software for North America for a company called Navision. Navision was a company that developed global financial software. Carl wanted to hire me to assist in the sales and marketing of the payroll and HR software for North America. This sounded so much better than the job I had. I jumped at the offer and terminated my position at Bellamy.

Life at home was busy. My son excelled at every sport he tried and we had him in soccer, baseball, hockey, and eventually lacrosse. My daughter was around six, so we started her in activities such as singing, dancing, swimming and gymnastics. We were running all over the place with the kids. The relationship with my husband was growing farther apart as we did not spend much time together and never made the effort to make the time. The open communication that we promised each other on our second marriage got lost in the mire of doing the best for our children.

CHAPTER 22

May 2002 to September 2004

Life in St. Albert

Working at Vision Pay was awesome. My mind was sharp. The people I worked with were extremely smart and we worked well as a team. About six months or so after I started, Microsoft purchased Navision and now we were the developers for the payroll and HR for North America for Microsoft Dynamics NAV. I flew in a private jet to meet with Microsoft executives in the US. It was amazing. I was at the top of my game.

Home life was up and down. I was still struggling with depression, seeing counselors and taking anti-depression drugs. Spirituality had not yet entered into my existence. I still pushed down things that hurt me. I still blew up at inappropriate times. I still hurt and had those lifelong beliefs of being unworthy. I had learned coping mechanisms from all of the therapists I had seen. I also had a strong realization of how speaking my truth, letting my voice be heard, allowing the feelings to come out, helps greatly in the healing process. However, due to the walls that were built between Rob and me, as well as the failed attempts to have my voice heard by him in the past, the speaking of my truth was to therapists. People who were paid to listen. I could not share my feelings with anyone else for fear they might judge me, look at me differently or shame me. When you talk to a therapist, they are paid to listen, paid not to judge. This is where I get my solace, from someone I pay.

We moved from St. Albert and purchased an acreage just outside of the city. It was beautiful. It was all set up for horses. Five acres backing up onto a tree and sod farm with an outside riding arena, a paddock, and a barn. You see, I have always had a huge love for horses. I used to bug my parents to no end to buy me a horse. This was a dream of mine. When we purchased the acreage, I went to a Pat Parelli clinic. I watched as I did not have a horse of my own. Pat taught natural horsemanship. I fell in love with his methods and came home with some of the tools he used. Then I purchased a saddle. Then I got my first horse, Monty. Monty was a tall thoroughbred, quarter horse cross. He was beautiful, but he had issues. I loved, and I groomed, and I rode him. I also got bucked off many, many times. I had a friend who was a Morgan horse breeder. I built a website for him. In payment I got my choice of that year's foals. I took my daughter out to his farm and I let her pick the foal. She also gave her the barn name Cheerios. I brought Cheerios and her mother back to the acreage. Her papered name was Two J Signature in Silk. I was in heaven with horses and I eventually ended up with four of them.

I have to say the years that I had my horses were some of my best years. I would come home after work and ride. I would wake up on cold winter mornings to go out and feed them. Walking on the crisp winter snow. Seeing the fog in the air. Hearing my horses nicker to me. It was the best feeling in the world! On the weekend, I would strap on my tool-belt and go and fix fences with my horses nuzzling me, asking what I was doing. I spent every moment I could with them, training them with natural horsemanship.

When I was young, I had this vision in my head. It was a vision of a beautiful house with kids in the country and a loving husband. It was a vision of peace and tranquility and happiness. This vision gave me strength during some of the hardest times in my life. When we got the acreage and I started working with my horses and my kids were happy, life was good. We had a happy family. One day, I was standing outside on the porch and it hit me. This was my vision, the vision of my youth, it had become reality. This vision that I had held within me all these years was now true. I exalted in this fact as the realization came to me and I floated for the rest of the day.

A week or two later, I came upon another realization. *If this vision is now my reality...What else is there?*

My husband soon started getting jealous of the time that I was spending with my horses. He was not happy with it. I never received any encouragement from him for what I was doing. Years later, we had an honest conversation and he acknowledged that he was jealous. He knew he was holding back praise. He would stand in the bedroom window and watch me work with my horses, seeing that I was doing wonderful work with them. However, he could never say that to me. It was stuck in his mind and there it would stay.

Rob and I had always been open with Michael regarding him having three sets of grandparents; that Rob had adopted him shortly after we were married. We went to see his paternal grandparents in Mexico at least every two years, and they could have contact with him when they wanted. His paternal father never tried contacting Michael. Michael had only seen pictures of Jeff on visits to Mexico to see his grandparents. At thirteen, Michael started telling Rob that he wasn't his real father, throwing it in his face. Although it hurt Rob, and me, when he said these things, we knew that it was a passing thing, something that all thirteen-year-olds went through.

Michael was into hockey full-time and traveling to tournaments was a common thing. There was a tournament close to where Jeff, his paternal father, lived. I told Rob that I did not want Michael meeting his paternal father without me being there. It was something I felt strongly about. This was a period in time that I went through with Michael and I wanted to be there to answer any questions that he had. It was extremely important for me to be there. I knew this from the bottom of my heart. I was not able to go to the tournament because of work. Rob took Michael and, without me knowing, set it up for Michael to meet Jeff. I learned after they got back that this happened. Another huge rock in the wall that was already so high I could not see past it. The complete and utter disregard for my feelings, as a mother, was totally and utterly unacceptable. There was no, "Sorry," no, "Please forgive me," nothing as he knew what he was doing when he did it, and he did not care how I felt about it.

CHAPTER 23

Fall 2004

Left Rob

Rob and I drifted far apart. I was unhappy. I gained a lot of weight. The wall had built up so much that I could not do it anymore. I could not be there anymore. We went to a counselor. I would sit there with my arms crossed not wanting to be there. She would send us home with homework. We needed to do something nice for the other person, whether we felt like it or not. We came back the next week and she asked what we had done. Rob started telling her all the things that he had done for me that week. He was proud, he completed his assignment. Then it was my turn to talk. I sat there, and I said I did nothing. Nothing at all. It was then I realized that I could not do this anymore. One of the reasons for not leaving before was the kids. But I thought I would rather have my kids grow up with two separate, happy parents than two parents that were unhappy together. I sat down with Rob and told him I was leaving, I wanted a divorce.

I moved out of the bedroom. I slept in the living room. We sat down one night, took out a piece of paper and separated all our belongings. It amazed me how easy it was to go through eleven years of belongings and divide them between us. We got an appraisal on the house and his dad gave him the money to buy me out. I purchased a house in St. Albert and moved out.

As soon as I made the decision to leave Rob, I had an influx of energy, extremely strong. It was like someone had turned a light bulb on. Not just a light bulb, but a bright stream of positively divine energy. I lost about fifteen to twenty pounds in a few weeks and became this brilliant bright light. Energy came back to me in spades. I had no idea what was happening, but I was happy, super happy, abnormally happy. I knew that the relationship ended because of communication issues between us. I made it a quest to determine how people communicate. The excess energy included excess sexual energy that I had no idea what to do with. I had not had any sexual energy for years now. This was exhilarating and confusing at the same time. I decided to pursue my quest for how people successfully communicate within the sexual world. The reason for this is that jealousy is one of the main factors of turmoil in a relationship. With that being said, there must be a great amount of communication between two people to overcome jealousy. That spurred my path into researching different aspects of communication that happen between people.

CHAPTER 24

2004 to 2005

A Sexual and Spiritual Awakening

I left Rob in October 2004, I was thirty-nine. I started going out dancing. I was not interested in any type of relationship or in men hitting on me. So I started going to the gay bar in downtown Edmonton. I never did have a lot of girlfriends and everyone I knew was still married, so I went out by myself. It was during the first time I went to the gay bar that I met Lonny J. He was in his early twenties and, of course, gay. He became my friend. He introduced me to his friends. It was a lot of fun because I forgot how much I loved dancing and it was all about dancing. I could dirty dance and not have anyone try to hit on me or take me home. I was given compliments that I could accept freely because I knew that they did not want anything else from me. I was happy. Each night I went out, I came home alone.

At home alone by myself for the first time in years. It was different, I became lonely, especially after all the dancing and music and action of the nightclub. Lonny and I hung out outside of the nightclub a few times. I remember he invited me over to his place for Easter supper. I brought my son with me as I wanted to introduce Michael to a different way of life. There was supposed to be another girl around his age joining us. However, she never made it. There we are sitting around the table having supper with openly gay men talking about the gay lifestyle in Edmonton. Michael, while behaving very well during the supper, was not very happy with me after as this was not something that he was used to. After all, he was a jock, active in all kinds of sports, especially hockey and lacrosse. Homosexuality was not something he was comfortable with. Ah well…we live and learn.

Fast forward to the present. Thirteen years after I met Lonny J. I see a post on Facebook saying that he had passed. He was a huge activist in the gay and lesbian community in Edmonton. He made friends wherever he went. He befriended me and made me feel comfortable. Even though his human form is gone I know that his soul has done well in this lifetime and I look forward to meeting up with him again when the time is right.

It was New Year's 2005, and I was thirty-nine. I had gone through so many changes in the past month, so I wanted to do something to celebrate. I decided to get a tattoo. Now I need to decide where I get the tattoo. This is something personal for me. I don't need to have anyone else see it. When I was living in Inuvik, I had a mole removed from my bum. I always scar badly so I thought I would get the tattoo to cover up the scar. Perfect! I go by myself to the tattoo parlor and I look through the books of tattoos. I decide on a stylized sun, thinking, *The sun does shine out of my ass.* Ha, ha. I lay down on the table and the tattoo artist asks where I want it. I point to a spot on my bum saying it's to cover up the scar. He does his work and sends me home with instructions on how to take care of it. I am looking in the mirror at his work and to my horror I see the scar on the other bum cheek. Oh no, I pointed to the wrong cheek. So now I have a scar on one side and a tattoo on the other. Sigh.

CHAPTER 25

2005

Caribbean Nude Cruise

Living alone part-time (as Rob and I were taking turns having the kids) gave me a lot of time to be by myself. I decided to catch up with people I had not spoken with for a while. One of these people was Rose. I had lost contact with her over the last six months or so. This petite, beautiful, sexy and smart woman and I were friends. I called her up and found out that she had just left her husband of many years, twenty-five years I think. We got together for lunch and hung out a bit. One day, she told me that she and Tom (her ex-husband) had purchased cruise tickets to the Caribbean, St. Martin, St. Thomas, St. Lucia and a few other places. It was a ten-day cruise. She was not going to go and wanted to give me her ticket. However, there were two things I needed to know. One—I would be going with Tom. She thought I would be good for him as I was lots of fun at that time and it would help him keep his mind off of her, and Two—this was a nudist cruise. As it turns out, they were nudists. They went on a nude cruise two years before. They had so much fun that they pre-purchased tickets for the next cruise. It was one of these tickets that she was now giving me. I did not know Tom all that well. I met him once at a company event. Rose invited me over for Boxing Day brunch in 2004 where we could meet and get to know each other better to determine if we wanted to go on the cruise together. I figured, out of 2,000 naked people on the boat, there had to be someone there that looked worse than me. Yes, I had issues. I decided to bite the bullet and go.

There was a chat board set up for people who were going on the cruise. I went in and looked at the chat threads. From what I could tell there were themed nights each night that included parades and parties. One of the first nights was a Mardi Gras night and there was a chat thread about body painting. This interested me. I looked at what was being written. I then decided to make a post: "I am willing to be painted, who wants to paint me?" This post initiated me in chatting with one of the people in my life who became paramount to my spiritual journey. His name was Donald and he was a massage therapist from the US. We start chatting and the topic of spirituality comes up. He recommends some books for me to read, *An Introduction to Paganism* and *The Ethical Slut* are two of the books that he recommends. I start reading the books and it gets interesting. I learn that there are different aspects to spirituality and that none of them are wrong. It is all how you perceive things. I am intrigued. I feel a shift in me. Intuitively it feels right.

Don and I chat on a continual basis before the cruise. I meet him in the lineup as we are waiting to get on the ship. He hangs with us, Tom and me, while the boat leaves the port. Everyone has to keep their clothes on until we reach international waters. I am anxious. Am I really doing this?

About forty minutes into the cruise the captain comes on the speaker system and says, "We have now entered international waters. Everyone can get undressed." *OMG*, I thought, *this is it.* I look around and everyone is taking off their clothes. *Well, if I leave my clothes on, everyone will stare.* So, I got undressed and then stood there embarrassed as I looked around and everyone was naked. It was not one of my best moments. Uncomfortable is how I feel, naked is how I look. I am amazed at myself for being able to push my limits and do this. I find out later on that there are only two people on the boat, other than the staff, who are fully dressed, that are not nudists. Me being one of them. So be it. After an hour or so I am more comfortable. I look around at all the naked people realizing that they do not care that I am naked.

There is something freeing about taking off a layer of the mask, one's clothes. You see, without the adornment of clothes you are taking away one of the main things that people use to judge you. You treat people differently when their stark naked reality hits you. I am more comfortable in my own skin now. Stretchmarks and scars do not matter for most people have them.

The second night is Mardi Gras night and there is a parade. I had already planned with Don that he would body paint me for the parade and I had purchased some gold body paint and brought along paint brushes. We are in his cabin, I am standing there, and he is painting my naked body. I allow him to use his artistic, creative abilities to paint whatever he wants. It is, I have to say, a little unnerving. The painting is taking a long time and we are running late. Don goes out into the hall and gets two more people to come in and help paint me. Now I have three people, two strangers and one I just met yesterday, painting my naked body. OMG!

The painting is done and we go down for the parade. Everyone is dressed up, or dressed down as this is a nudist event…lol. There are some amazing costumes. I feel very uncertain and uncomfortable, my anxiety is on high alert and my voice gets lost. I have never been happy with my body and my babies have left me with lots of stretchmarks and my breasts have seen better days as I breastfed both babies. Oh well, suck it up, princess, and just go with it. My mind is chattering all the time, lots of negative chatter. *You are not good enough, what are you doing? You are making a fool of yourself.* I push those comments to the side. I have people stopping me and telling me how amazing I look. I am confused as the little voice in my head denies it all. Part of the parade is walking across the stage while people in the audience watch and clap. I am aghast, in a fog, not knowing what I am doing there. But I do it all the same. Take a deep breath and walk across that stage. All I am wearing is gold paint, my body is the canvas. It was surreal. I have tapped into that inner strength that knows I can do anything. My little voice is being shoved aside now.

The day after the parade, I have several people coming up to me and talking to me, saying they saw me last night and how brilliant I looked. My voice hears the compliments and does not allow me to acknowledge them. I cannot say, "Thank you," as my mind will not let me believe it. I know now that this is the "I am not worthy" part of my belief system that will not allow a compliment to be acknowledged. My little voice says, *Yeah, its not me you are talking to. You have to be mistaken.* Many years later, I have learned how to tame that voice so as to hear a compliment, acknowledge it from my heart and to truly say thank you. For who am I to take someone's truth and treat it as a lie?

There is an area on the ship that has vendors selling their wares. I walk around and take a look. One of the vendors is doing some kind of spiritual drawings of people. Her name is Sofanya and she is from Big Sur, California. She takes a piece of paper and sprays it with water. She then meditates on you for about ten minutes. The meditation tells her what colors of paint to use. She takes the paint and drops them on different areas of the paper. Because the paper is wet the paint colors start running into each other. Once done she asks me to blow on the paint, and they run into each other further.

It is kind of like a tie dye effect. She makes the comment that she is rarely told to use the color gold and it surprises her as there is quite a bit of gold on the paper. Once this is done she allows the paint to dry and then starts drawing. She is seeing things in the patterns of the paint and these are the things she draws. She also includes a drawing of your face. The result is simply amazing. Each and every time I look at this picture I see different things; animals, waterfalls, fairies, hearts, a dove, a brilliant red bird with a long neck, a golden lion, a golden goddess with her hand on the tree of life, a wise Chinese man, a dolphin and more. I LOVE IT! At my third eye , where my scar is on my forehead, there is a huge heart with the universe inside, stars and a galaxy. This picture has been with me everywhere I go. I still look at it today in awe and amazement. It reminds me that I am more than what I think. It reminds me of the magnificence of my being.

I have my birthday on the cruise. I turn forty. Don is a sweetheart. He makes reservations for me at the restaurant. He buys me supper, he treats me really well. I am swelling with happiness.

One day, while the ship is out at sea, Don and I are sitting in his cabin and talking. We are discussing spirituality and communication and my difficulty in not being able to communicate, how words get stuck in my throat and I am unable to allow them out. He folds me in his arms, my back to his chest, and tells me that he is going to give me the space to do some free flow speaking. He instructs me how to do this. It does not matter what I say or how I say it, my job is just to talk, not to think, to continue speaking about whatever pops into my head no matter what it is. His job is to hold me, to hold space for me, non-judgmentally, and allow me to speak without him commenting. *Hmm...*I start slowly, my mind is present and it is deciding on what to say. I start, I stop, I stutter and then I give in, I release my thinking brain and just talk. I say whatever comes up. The good, the bad, the ugly, the sorrow, the pain. I am crying and talking and, when I need it, I get a squeeze, a hug, a confirmation that I am doing well without him saying anything. The energy in the room changes. It becomes electric as the words tumble out of me. This went on for an hour or two. I have no remembrance of what I said. After I was done, I felt fatigued and tired, so many things were said, but not with just words, also with emotions and feeling. He kissed me, told me that I did amazing and then we laid down on his bed and he held me and kissed me until I fell asleep. When we woke up, it was late and dinner had already started. I felt surreal like I was floating. One of the rules on the boat was that you had to wear something when going out for supper, so I put on a long, white shirt of his. We went for supper, Don walking and me floating beside him. I felt people staring at me. I felt like there was this white aura radiating around me. People stopped us and commented on how beautiful I looked. I just smiled as I had no more words to say. I just felt peace.

A few days into the cruise Don came up to me and said that there were a couple of men on board who wrote for a nudist magazine, specializing in nudist travel. It was called *Travel Naturally.* They had written an article on the old nudists not being very happy with the new nudists coming in with tattoos and piercings. In any case, they were looking for some people who had tattoos and piercings for a photo shoot to go along with this article. Don asked me if I wanted to be in the photo shoot. It was at this time that I had recently gotten the tattoo on my bum and, of course, I am always trying to find things to get me out of my shell, so I said, "Why not?" We did the photo shoot and they took my name and address. About four or five months later, I got an envelope in the mail. It consisted of the magazine. The article with an accompanying picture was about midway through the magazine. There I was with my back, butt and face smiling along with six or so other nudists.

I took walks by myself on the cruise ship, just to find places where I could sit and relax without a lot of people around. I was sitting upstairs somewhere, and this guy came up to talk to me. His name was Larry. He had seen me around the ship as well as on Mardi Gras night. We had a wonderful conversation and he was very intrigued about this being my first time as a nudist. I was as uncomfortable as always talking to new people as I have never been good at small talk and get nervous. Larry was good because he led most of the conversation. He and I have kept in touch throughout the years, at one point, we were even in the same city, in the US, and met up for dinner. He also came down to Playa del Carmen on vacation and we spent a couple of days together. Nothing ever occurred with Larry other than friendship. I am grateful for that as I had become very wary of men and kept my distance as much as possible. This was due to my past and me thinking if I was great in bed then someone would love me, which is what happened when everyone used me as I did not have the confidence in myself to think I was worth it otherwise. I made the decision that I was to be wary of men.

There is one more point that I would like to add with regards to going on a nude cruise. Make sure to bring stretchy pants for when leaving the ship. On cruises you get access to food 24/7; without the need for clothes one tends not to watch what they are eating and thus can gain weight, such as I did when I found out that I could not do up my jeans on the last day.

CHAPTER 26

November 14, 2017

An Update into Present Life...

I just received an email from Graham, my father. I have not heard from him in a few years. The subject of the email is *Hello my DAUGHTER*, yup, in caps. The *To:* line is to someone called *Carla Pheagan*—does he not know how to spell my name? The content of the email is exactly as follows:

> DEAR CARLA, How are you?? much time has gone by since we last communicated and this is something that I feel I need to address while I am able to. The purpose of this email is to express to you my deep inner feelings about the past rollercoaster life that I have had and I now realize that I have been responsible for much distress within my family. To that end, I feel that since I AM able to, express my regrets and misgivings to all of my family for not being the perfect parent and father. I have recently celebrated my 79 th birthday and am living with July my male cat and November my golden lab dog in a cabin on the north bank of a mountain stream since 1999, and if all goes well, this is where I will live the rest of my life. To YOU MY ONLY DAUGHTER, I wish to let you know

that I often think about you and LOVE YOU DEARLY. I cannot change the past and am having to live with my regrets which I will be taking to the grave with me. I sincerely hope that I have not poured salt into old wounds. I wish you and your family WELL. LOVE, Graham.

I am not sure how to take this. Graham reaches out every once in a blue moon, well, a little less than that. This is my chance to walk the talk. But oh, it is so much harder to do than to say. I, at this moment, am struggling with a bit of depression. I am working my way through it, giving myself small tasks to do every day, being easy on myself, finding the good in life, and writing. Truth be told, the writing, which is allowing me to release past hurts, also brings up the constant unhappiness that I have felt throughout my existence. This is a lesson I am still learning, to live life in the now and in bliss. I know that it is coming, I feel it. My writing is cathartic, and it allows my logical mind to put pieces together, to see where the past beliefs were put into place. To see how they were solidified into my being. To understand the true me who has the strength to pick myself up and keep going. To keep myself alive. To not give in. To live my life's purpose as I have always felt that there was a purpose. To let go of the old. To allow the new to permeate me. No, not the new, to allow the truth of who I AM to become present in all of its glorious splendor.

I know that I am not able to answer right away. I need to allow myself the ability to let go of the words. The response, if I do decide to respond, will come when it is ready.

Surprise, surprise, poetry arises…

Sperm Donor 2

Oh, sperm donor,
I do see
how you live your life alone
with your memories.

After seventy-nine years of living life
only now you understand
that the life you thought worth living
has come crashing all around.

Why did it take such a long time
to understand what has been done?
To regret what you once thought was right
as you were a selfish one.

Do a few words take away
all the pain
and heartache
that was given so freely
to ME, YOUR ONLY DAUGHTER?

I should be the better person,
forgive and understand;
I will be the better person
for the damage that was done.

The wounds still seem so raw,
open and bleeding, you see,
as I still do remember
how it all made me feel.

The life of living
with not being loved,
the lessons burned so deeply
in the basement of my life.

I found the inner strength
to give the love I needed,
to hold myself,
to hug myself,
to love unconditionally.

Now I must dig deep
to go beyond the pain and hurt,
to forgive and understand
the lessons that have been taught.

For life has not been easy,
we do what we think we must.
Based on the beliefs and pain
from past disdain
we make the choices,
we take the blame.

Do I now talk freely?
Open up my soul to you
To tell how I am feeling?
For I think it will damage you.

This is my struggle
for my truth will hurt you
and I do not want to hurt you
for I know how it feels.

Karma is a bitch,
it comes around, you see;
you treat someone like shit
you will get shit back...
times three.

Where is my compassion?
Where is my empathy?
For a lost soul such as yours.
They have been lost throughout the years
of not being loved or cared for...
at all.

I feel you reaching out to me,
I feel the pain you are in
do I put on the mask
to ease that pain
or tell you the truth
of how I feel?

I am in a silent confusion,
not knowing what to do.

Response to Graham
I have had time to think.
I have had time to cry.
I have had time to lick my wounds,
to think about what I must do.

I must be true to me,
to the person I have become.
I will not lie,
I will not put on the mask

to make you feel
fine at last.

I will respond
in email form
to let you know
what I must say.

A father you call yourself,
that is a lie,
a lie you tell yourself
for why?
I cannot try
to understand.

A proposed email response to Graham:

Hello Graham,

I read your email. In all honesty I am not sure what you want from me. All I can do is tell you my truth of what I am thinking in the here and now. You were never a father, nor part of a family. This I think you know to be true. My memories of you are not good ones. I actually cannot remember any good of the little time that you were around me. I have come to terms that I never had a father. Not in the true sense of the word. A father is a word that is deserving of someone who loves their offspring, who spends time with them, who gets to know them. Who actually knows how to spell their last name, as I have had the same last name for about twenty-five years now.

What love I had for you was the love of a daughter who so desperately needed and wanted a father to love her back. I since understand that it was all hope and need from my part as that love was never there from you.

I am sorry if these words feel harsh to you. But in all sincerity, I have no idea who you are. The love for you was lost in the years of neglect.

Carla Feagan
P.S. Now you know how to spell my last name at least.

I never did send the email. Instead I chose to say nothing. I am in a quandary about this, about sending a response. Why do we have such bonds to the people that helped make us? Why do we feel that we have to keep them in our lives when they so obviously left us out of theirs? What is it that makes us keep trying to gain the approval of someone who treated us so wrong? These are the questions I ask myself. This is the confusion I find myself in. The spiritual side of me says to forgive, to understand. But does that mean that I have to allow people who have treated me wrong back into my life, back into my existence? I have come to a forgiveness and an understanding about my mother as I have learned some of her past and I knew what she went through. As for my father, I can forgive what was done. My only understanding is that he never had the capability of being a father as he was too self-centered. Why do I want to have a relationship with him now? So I decide to stay silent. To say nothing. Not send the response I so carefully wrote. Some may think this is right, others may think it is wrong. It is for me to decide and do what I think is best for me based on my heart and my soul.

CHAPTER 27

2005

BDSM

During my quest to determine how people successfully communicate, I get put in touch with a man, Ronald, who is into BDSM. BDSM stands for bondage, dominance, submission and masochism. The book *Fifty Shades of Grey* brought a bit of light into the BDSM world. I give Ronald a call and ask to meet with him and his partner to have a discussion on BDSM and the need to be able to communicate with your partner. As it turns out, Ronald makes floggers. A flogger has a handle and a bunch of leather or suede or horsehair throngs attached to it. One takes the flogger and in a rhythmical method flogs the other person. The intent does not have to be to mark or hurt someone. In actuality a flogger handled by a professional can feel like a really good massage.

I explained to Ronald that I was on the search to discover how people communicate effectively with each other. In my mind, sex can cause concerns in communication. When thinking about BDSM, I surmised that there has to be a lot of communication in order to trust someone to do the things that are done in that realm. Ronald taught me about safe words and some of the things that can occur in a BDSM relationship. He also suggested that I attend a yearly event that the BDSM community has. It includes sessions on different topics surrounding this lifestyle. I am honored that he so easily answers all of my questions and allows me to take part in this event. He knows full well that this is not a lifestyle that I choose to be in and therefore have no intent on "joining in".

There is a trade show there where one can purchase things, as well as an entertainment night where one can partake in activities in a closed off area, or just mingle, and meet and greet other people of like mind. Of course I am going to go! Well, I have to say it was an eye-opener for me. It is one thing to hear or read or talk but another altogether to see. My mind was a little blown as I am not really into the BDSM scene. However, I do not make any judgments of people who are. The way I see it is, if there are two consenting adults and no one is getting hurt—well, at least those who don't want to be hurt—who am I to say if it is right or wrong?

Ronald has a booth there selling his floggers. He asks me if I want to try and he promises he will not hurt me. Umm, OK. I bend over and he starts flogging me. It feels good, it's like a massage. I am confused. "Is it not supposed to hurt?" I ask.

He says, "No, but it can if you want it to."

He was just being easy on me. OK I get it.

CHAPTER 28

2005 to 2006

Single Again

The first couple of years of being single after eleven years of marriage were quite a trial and error in figuring out what it was that I wanted. I knew that I did not want a serious relationship, and I was wary of men taking advantage of me. But I had this huge sexual energy that was coursing through my body. I am not good at picking up men, never have been, probably never will be. That is fine with me. A friend at work suggested internet dating. I had heard about it, but never did any research into it. I asked if he knew of any websites. He suggested Ashley Madison. Well, I go on and create a profile and start chatting with these men. They seemed kind of slimy to me. A bit later, I found out that the site was geared towards married men who want to cheat on their wives. I immediately took down my profile. Totally not what I wanted.

Time to try a different site. I think it was Plenty of Fish. OMG, the first time I got on it was crazy. So many men, such little time. Until I realized that there are a lot of men who just want to chat and will never meet. Other men will meet reluctantly, and then you find out that they look nothing like the pictures they posted. Still others will meet in person and they look like their picture, but there is absolutely nothing there as far as chemistry. So many men, so many failed attempts.

I had not actually had sex with anyone yet, but I had the full intention of doing so. I asked a male co-worker if he would go to the drug store with me and help pick out condoms as I have never had to do that either. I wanted to be safe. At lunch we went out and had a lot of fun deciding what condoms to purchase. I had no idea that there were so many different types. It was like, "Well, if I get the extra large, will it intimidate the man?" or, "Does the ribbed really make a difference?" or, "Ooh...look, this one is scented... huh?"

I was finally taking control of my life and deciding what I wanted. It felt good. I ended up having a couple of relationships with younger men who were infatuated with older women. This was perfect for me as I felt extremely sexy and wanted, and there was no chance of a full time relationship happening. These men were not just used for sex either. They were smart and funny and we had a great time inside and outside of the bed. It appeased my mind. The best thing, they were typically at my beck and call.

These relationships were good in the beginning, but I felt like I was missing something. I started to crave the companionship of another being, of a man. Not just the sex. Life also started getting a little lonely. As stated above, I am no good at starting up conversations with people, especially people I may take a liking to. I did not want to meet someone in a bar, and there were no men approaching me in the grocery store or at the gym. So I switched dating sites and set up a profile on Match.com as I was told that there were more men on there who were serious about relationships. Back I go into online dating hell.

Actually, it was not that bad. Even though I did not meet anyone as far as boyfriend material is concerned, I did meet a couple of men who became great friends and we are still in touch today. One of these men, Rene, ended up connecting me with many beautiful, spiritual souls throughout the years. Rene is a unique man with a unique past and lots of connections to spiritual people. He creates energy pendants and energy boards based upon a technology in the Quantum Vortex. Don't ask me what that means. I have had many conversations with Rene on his technology and how it does what it does. However, as of today, it still eludes me. All I know is what I feel when I have these pendants and boards around. The energy is there, it is real. Throughout my journey, this is one fact that I am sure of, we are all energy and we are all interconnected.

In 2005, my brother Mark gets married. I go down to the wedding. I have met his wife, Angela, a couple of times before and we get along well. The more time passes and the more I get to know Angela the closer we become. Today we are spiritual soul sisters. She is this powerful, beautiful woman with lots of drive. We have had many eye-opening conversations as well as card readings together as she does card readings for fun. She has been there for me throughout a lot of my trials and tribulations, most of which have dealt with relationships, the triggers that make me fall back into past beliefs. She has given me an open, non-judgmental, compassionate space to allow my words to flow so that I can release. I do not know where I would be if I did not have her compassionate ear.

Near the end of 2006, I am a bit disgruntled. I have ended the relationships with the young men as that need has been sated and I would like a little more. Online dating is frustrating, many one-time dates with no sparks. VisionPay is now called Serenic as it merged with a US company, and upper management has changed. There are things that I am not happy with that came from these changes, so I feel it is time that I leave. But hey, I have broken my two-year mark;

I have been with this company for close to five years. My spiritual belief system is growing in spurts. I have no anger flare-ups as there is no one to trigger me. I am starting to feel lonely and with that comes the sadness of not being wanted, of not being worthy.

CHAPTER 29

January 2007 to March 2009

Relationships

I start a new job working for Open Door Technology. It is still with the software that I was working with at Serenic, Microsoft Dynamics NAV. However, I am in a different role. I no longer specialize in payroll and HR; I am looking after the education vertical, selling into school boards. I have much to learn as I now need to know the full accounting package as well as the special requirements for school boards. My mind is sated as it likes new challenges.

I decide to try internet dating again. I get into a relationship, it is with a man who likes to have control. He treats me well, he buys me things, we travel a bit. I am his pawn, and for the meantime I am OK with it. It is much better than being lonely. However, this is not a good relationship to have with someone who has my past experiences. I get triggered; I flare up; I come crashing down; I am sorry. I get hooked; I cannot leave; I become obsessive; I become jealous. I forget about spirituality. The relationship lasts less than a year, but it has done damage and I have fallen into an abyss. For days I cry, I cannot get over him, I cannot think about anything else other than him. I do realize that he is not good for me but those past beliefs, the needing, the wanting, they arise like a flame from a fire burning too bright. I need to talk; I need to get these voices out of my head; I need to give them light. My Angela, my dear, dear Angela, listens to me, listens to my rants, listens to my ravings, allows me to speak, and then offers some advice, offers understanding, offers compassion, offers love. She is there for me to assist me in picking myself up off the floor and realizing how strong I am.

I lick my wounds for the next few months. I come to an understanding of what this relationship did to me, of what I allowed it to do to me. I get back on my spiritual path. I meditate and give myself space and love and compassion. I find me again. I come to an understanding of how it happened, what allowed it to happen. I am learning about me and my past and how it affects me. I survive, and a piece of me gets put into place.

I am whole again, but the loneliness creeps back in. For someone who has spent so much time alone one would think I would be used to it. But no, I still need something, need someone to make me feel complete. Back to the Internet I go. I go on a date with Dan. He is nice and talks a lot so I do not have to worry about keeping the conversation going. We have a couple of dates, he drops me off at home and we have a kiss. Nothing more. He invites me to go away with him for a weekend. It is beautiful, he is kind and funny and smart and we get along well together. We date for a couple of years. I really like his family and it is comfortable. Nonetheless, my demons are lurking inside, waiting for the right moment, waiting for the trigger, patiently waiting. You see, what I did most of the time, when I felt hurt, I would push it down, not say anything, not want to rock the boat. This is not good as those feelings compile and get added to the demons that are waiting. When the right moment comes, all those feelings get pushed out alongside the past beliefs. Except those past beliefs have gone from sadness to anger. *I am worthy and why should I put up with this? Fuck you for making me feel this way.*

While my feelings do have merit, I do not deal with them correctly. Rather than give them a voice when they arise, I push them down, so when I do get triggered, it all comes out in anger. I am not proud of this. I do not like this. This is not me. I understand this now, I have learned those lessons. But back then not so much. I had not yet learned to give voice to what was happening in the present. I was mean, and I blamed, and I brought up all the feelings of hurt in one big, long diatribe. Of course, when someone is attacked, they fight back. So while my feelings may have come from a place of truth, the way that they came out pushed us apart.

I did have a lot of fun with Dan, we were good together. It was me that pushed us apart by not knowing how to talk about my feelings in a manner that created compassion and understanding. Nothing ever got resolved, because how could something be resolved in a fit of anger? I have learned these lessons in my here and now. It took fifty years to learn these lessons. Even after we broke up, Dan was there for me, and I was there for him. A love will always reside in my being for this man.

CHAPTER 30

2009

Life Lessons

I would like to take the time to explain a couple of important life lessons that I have learned and started putting into play.

I learned to take ownership of my own feelings, to stop blaming other people for how I feel. You see, in the past, I used to blame others for making me feel a certain way. However, I now realize this is wrong. Others do not have your experiences, your past beliefs, they do not know what triggers you, what makes you react. When I realized this, I looked back at some of the things that I got hurt from or became angry at. I saw, when looking deep into myself, that the hurt or the anger typically came from a past belief within me. It made a huge impact on me. Looking internally rather than externally for a cause turned my life around, so much so that I started looking internally for everything. I took on the blame for everything; I got confused as to whether the feelings were mine to look after, or if there was something that I actually should be hurt or angry about. I swung from one end of the pendulum to the other.

In the end, I did find a balance, I became much more aware of what is my shit and what is someone else's shit. I learned to deal with my own shit, in my own way, by identifying the root cause of the belief, of the hurt, going deep into myself, discovering what I needed at the time of the original hurt or belief. Was it love, was it compassion, was it just someone holding me? Whatever it was, I gave it to myself, I sat there in tears, I felt the pain, I gave myself the thing that I needed at the time, my love, my compassion, my empathy. This, for me, helps peel away a layer of the onion.

As I was learning not to project my stuff onto other people, I became aware of other people projecting their stuff onto me. I could see myself taking their stuff personally, bringing it into my being, trying to fix it, to make it better. I learned how to decipher where things were coming from, was it me or was it them, did it even involve me? My intuitive self had grown during the process of taking blame for everything. It needed to grow in order to be able to balance myself and take a look at circumstances in a different light. I became aware that, like me, people have their own stuff to work through, and, like me, they need to understand and realize it and stop projecting. I stopped allowing people to project their stuff onto me. I did this in a warm, loving way, by opening space, allowing them to talk, allowing myself to talk, and by setting up my limits and boundaries. I am not saying to tell the other person to go off and deal with it themselves. If they need help I would be there for them. But I was not going to allow it to affect me, just as I do not expect anyone to take in my stuff. I can ask for help, but I do not project the feelings of anger and hurt on to anyone else anymore. Well, at least I try and I am aware. I am human and I do falter, but I usually figure it out soon after and try to make things right.

CHAPTER 31

March 2009 to September 2011

Divine Body Spa

Open Door started laying off people in December 2008. I am one of the people let go in the third round of layoffs, which would have been in March 2009. In the previous months I had been having conversations with an ex-boyfriend. He formed the idea of starting a laser hair removal shop with him. I had been researching this idea for a couple of months and it seemed like a viable concept. When I got laid off, I was OK with it as I was ready for a change. What a wonder, I had been working there for two years. Anyways, when I got laid off, it took me two days to decide that I was going to move forward with opening my own business. First thing I needed to do was to create a business plan and get funding. The laser machine we were looking at was quite expensive. When I was about three quarters done with the business plan, I decided that I did not want to be partners with my ex. I told him that and we lost touch for the next couple of years.

I changed the business plan to include spa services and I did research to find services that were unique. I finished the business plan, got the funding, found the location, hired the staff, decided on the products to introduce, and got training on the new equipment, as well as becoming certified as a laser technician. All of this in just two months. I officially opened the doors to Divine Body Spa in May of 2009. I was focused and energized and stressed and worked 24/7.

The spa was open for two and a half years and I worked nonstop. My typical day was to get up, go to the spa, work, come home, normally around nine pm, do laundry for the spa and go to bed. I did this for two and a half years straight. It took all my time, my energy, and, alas, my money. However, I met many spiritual people, had many experiences and learned a LOT! This was also the time period when people from all over kept telling me I was a healer. The paragraphs below are stories of some of the people I met and experiences I had.

Sophie—I met Sophie the same year that I opened my spa. She was a brilliantly beautiful person. I would give her treatments and we would spend time talking about everything. Sophie is still a very good friend of mine, one of my soul sister tribe. Being a wonderfully spiritual person, many of our conversations had to do with our beliefs and how they affect our lives. She had been on a spiritual path for a long time. There was one woman who she saw quite often to assist her in her spiritual growth. Her name was Irene. Sophie raved about this person and what she was doing for her. I decided to give it a go and I went to see her. The first thing Irene said to me was, "You are a healer."

I said, "Yeah, I don't think so." I had a huge block in believing this. While she seemed true to me regarding what she was saying or doing, I did not have the feeling that I needed to see her again.

This is one thing that I have learned. There are many different forms of spirituality out there, many teachers and much learning. What one needs to do is to listen to one's own being to determine if what one is hearing or reading intuitively feels right for them. There is no right or wrong when it comes to what you believe or what does not feel right for you. It is a personal feeling, a personal preference. To listen to one's own instincts, I believe, is the way to go. It is like being in front of a smorgasbord. We don't eat everything. We pick and choose what we like and what looks good and what feels right.

A few years later, when I was living in Playa del Carmen, Sophie gave me a call and told me that she was getting married. I was very happy for her and I planned to be there on her wedding day. It was beautiful, and I was very happy to have been there on this special day for her. For the dinner, I was seated at the table with Irene. It had been a few years since I had seen her, and I had only seen her the one time. She sat down and looked at me and her smile grew wide. She remembered me. She told me that my energy was a LOT stronger than it was before, my aura was glowing and that I had many spirit guides around me who were looking after me. God shivers went throughout my body as she was talking. For me, when I hear truth, I mean deep-seated, intuitive truth, I get an energy rush throughout my entire body. I call these god shivers. I thanked her deeply and told her that it was a blessing to have seen her again.

Sherry—Sophie told me about this person who came and did a group session at Irene's. Her name was Sherry. I am not entirely sure what it was that they did, but it was definitely spiritual in nature, and Sophie was very impressed, so impressed that she had a personal tarot card reading with Sherry. At that time, Sherry lived in Red Deer and came up to St. Albert to do readings. I was intrigued, and a little lost and forlorn with the way the spa was going. I made an appointment with Sherry for a reading. I remember this as clear as if it were yesterday. Sherry was staying in a hotel, so I knocked on her room door. As soon as she opened the door I got god shivers running throughout my body. She introduced herself and we sat down. There was beautiful music in the background, and she recorded the reading. I shuffled the cards and she placed them down. The first thing she said was, "You are a healer."

I thought, *OMG, not this again…Whatever.* Throughout the reading, when she said something that felt right, I would get god shivers. The entire reading, I was having god shivers. There were two other important things that she said during the reading, which have stuck with me throughout my later years. The first, she saw me above the earth. I am a brilliant white light. From the center of my being I had brilliant white streams of light going all over the world. She said that I was put on this planet at this time to help, to assist people, to assist the world in moving towards the new paradigm, the new energies that were coming into the world. My purpose is much larger than me. I need to know it. The second thing she said was that I needed to write a book. A book of my life. This would assist me in what I had to do. You see, at this point in my life, my old belief system of not being worthy, of being less than, was still inherently strong and powerful. I could not see myself as this being that she talked about. I also did not see myself writing a book. *Really, me, I can't do that, I don't know how.*

Sherry and I kept in touch and became friends. More than friends, I truly believe she was brought into my life to assist and guide me. Sherry was the person who taught me that being a healer does not have to do with healing in the traditional sense. I spent a weekend with her in Red Deer. It was like being with the universe. As we were having conversations she would all of a sudden go quiet and then say, "OK, I have been told to tell you this," or, "They told me to tell you…" and then words of wisdom would flow from her. One day, we were sitting at the back of a restaurant talking about what had happened in our lives. Sherry, you see, has had a hard life and she was looking for some wisdom for herself.

She forced me to go deep inside and to channel for her. The

mind was there instantly: *You cannot do this, you do not know how, who do you think you are?* All the negative programming from my experiences was there. However, at this point, Sherry and I had this surreal energy around us and she was able to assist in pushing me through this negative self-talk, to go into my heart, to open up my intuitive self, and to channel wisdom for her. I put my mind aside and allowed the wisdom to flow through me. I sat there with god shivers and tears, and answered the questions that she had. I came to a realization that when I speak truth, I cry. Tears flow down my face. I get in this amazing place of calm. My beautiful friend had allowed me to see that my healing does not come from a place of touching or putting hands on someone, such as reiki or massage; it comes from my inner being, my inner voice. I have the ability to listen, non-judgmentally, with compassion and empathy and, if necessary, to be able to allow the wisdom to flow from me. I am in awe. I also realized that everything that I have gone through has given me the experience and knowledge of the feelings that arise during hard and turbulent times. This allows the energy of knowing, the energy of being non-judgmental, and the energy of empathy, of compassion, to flow freely in a warm, loving space. For what we all want, what we all need, is to allow ourselves to speak our truth to a non-judgmental, compassionate ear and, most of all, to be heard, to have someone understand the hurt behind the words. For to let the words out, to allow the emotions to release, brings in the light to set us free. It is the holding on to the words and pushing them down that brings darkness into us. We keep these deadly secrets deep down inside as they are bad, they are wrong, people will look at us differently, people will see us differently. I know this feeling, I have been there. I have been blessed enough to have opened up to people who give me the space to speak my truth. I have felt the bliss after the words came out. I have also tried opening up to people who were not there for me and I know the devastating feeling of not being understood, of being judged or triggering the other person so that they react and move away.

We all have these deep-seated feelings that we think we cannot talk about. I am here to listen, to understand, to allow those feelings to be heard and to be released. Is it an easy process? No, it is not. Is it a fast process? Not at all. Because these feelings, these emotions, have been with us for a very long time. It will not take one day to get rid of them. I look back at my life through the writing of these memoirs and I see where the initial beliefs were ingrained in me. I also see all the things that happened in my life that added to these beliefs, that solidified them, that made them true to me. The thing is we just need to start, to reach out and speak, to let these feelings out, peel away the layers of the beliefs so they weaken. Each time you speak your truth, a layer gets peeled away. One day, you will wake up and that belief will have no more control over you. It still may be there, but it is an afterthought, not ruling you as it once did. This is why we are here, to learn to let go of the past to be able to live fully within ourselves.

It was via Sherry where all the messages about me writing a book came through. It was the universe, my spirit guide, guardian angels, I have no idea what to call them, that was speaking through Sherry. Each time I had a reading with her I would be told the same thing, I needed to write.

Jacinta—My dearest Jacinta. She came into the spa with two of her children, both grown adults, to look at some of our services. I spent a lot of time with them, answering all the questions that they had. She booked some services for her son and then some for herself. We spoke endlessly during her services. We became fast friends. We talked about spirituality and our lives, our experiences. It was beautiful. She is beautiful and smart and funny and has an amazing energy. A soul sister to the truest extent. She could feel me. She could tell when I was upset even if she was nowhere near me.

A story of Jacinta feeling me…

Nyceim, who I will write about next, was living with me and I was diving deep into the rabbit hole of spirituality with him. One day, I had gone to a crystal, rock, and spiritual shop with Sophie and the girl at the front desk took one look at me and said, "You are a healer." My mind tumbled down the hole of not believing again, so we dropped the subject. She told Sophie and me that we had past lives together, one of them as princesses in Egypt. Intuitively, it felt like truth as Sophie and I had become very close, very fast. She also said that I had a lot of anger in me, anger that needed to be released. She said that she had a specific meditation that would allow the anger to come out and be released. I am standing there thinking, *I am not angry, I do not feel angry, if anything I am the opposite of angry, I am burned out, I am tired, but anger…no way.* However, I had a feeling inside that there was some truth to this, so I went back and had the meditation session. After the session, she told me to be careful within the next few days as the anger may come out at any time. I was to give myself space to allow it and release it. I had already planned on going away for the weekend with Nyceim to Waterton Lakes National Park, a well-deserved getwaway for me. I bought some incense and a Shiva Lingam stone to bring along on the journey.

Shiva Lingam is a sacred stone from India. This stone holds within it the feeling of unity and duality. You have the masculine part of the stone within its phallic shape and the feminine as well in the egg shape. The stone resonates that it is one, yet there are two separate entities within the one, masculine and feminine.

At certain times in my life I have seen something in a store and I look at it and think, *Ah, there you are, you are mine, I found you,* so I automatically pick it up and purchase it. I did that with the Shiva Lingam. The next day, Nyceim and I drive down to Waterton. We get into the hotel room and it is beautiful. There is a beautiful bathroom and I decide to take a nice, hot bath as the drive was long. Nyceim went for a nap. I felt like I needed to de-stress so I created a blissful environment. I smudged the room with sage to cleanse it. I lit incense; I ran a nice, hot bath and put essential oils in it. I lit candles. Then I went and laid in the bath. It was heaven. Then my mind started whirling and I started feeling anxious, I got very agitated. I got out of the bath and immediately started a fight with Nyceim. In the back of my head I am thinking, *WTF is going on?* It was as if I had no control. The anxious, angry feeling lasted the entire weekend. I had no idea what was going on. Nyceim took the brunt of it. I managed to settle down a bit on the ride home. As soon as I arrived back home, I received a call from Jacinta. She asked me what happened on Friday night. She continued to say that she was in a business meeting in Banff and she could feel me. She could feel all the anger coming from me. She sent me healing, calming energy. She sensed when I was back and needed to find out what occurred. I told her about the meditation and Nyceim, and what transpired on Friday night and throughout the weekend. Together we figured it out. The meditation had opened up the part of me that was angry. When I went to Waterton, I set up a safe spiritual environment, which allowed my inner self to let the anger out. And come out it did. As soon as we realized what happened, I immediately felt better. I had a talk with Nyceim to tell him what had happened and to ask for forgiveness as it was not related directly to him.

Jacinta has been there for me, feeling me, sending me loving energies from the time that we met. I feel very blessed to have her as a soul sister.

Nyceim—December 2010 to July 2011. Wow, what a wild ride

we had! You came into my life for a purpose and that purpose included high highs and low lows. I am blessed to still have you within my soul tribe. It was December 20, 2010. I was working in the spa. I lead a solo existence, so I decide to try online dating again. I started chatting with this guy online, Nyceim. He was handsome and smart and spiritual. We decide to meet for drinks. I go to the lounge and he is sitting there, just as handsome as in the pictures. We start talking and it is easy, like a breath of fresh air. As we are talking I look at his phone and he has this sticker on it. I know the sticker as my friend Rene sells them and I have one on my phone as well. I ask him about it and he knows Rene. We also discover that we were at the same meeting a month or so ago. It was a meeting that I went to with Rene. We start talking about spirituality. He has been on the spiritual path for a few years, so much so that it has changed him and his way of thinking. His wife and best friend of many, many years could not understand the changes happening in him and so their marriage became estranged. He was still living with her in their house, he was in the basement in a separate room. We start talking about the spiritual significance of December 21, the winter solstice. We make a plan to meet at my place after work the next day to write a note of our wants or needs in life, light a fire outside, and burn them in a spiritual ceremony. I am exited and happy and have renewed energy from this new person who has entered my life.

The next day, December 21, 2010, I am driving to work. It is a beautiful, sunny, clear and cold morning. I am on the phone to my mother talking excitedly about my plans for the night. I tell her about the solstice and the fire and the ceremony I am planning to do. All of a sudden, I see a rainbow in the sky and then get a huge energy rush throughout my body. I immediately start crying. I hang up the phone and have to pull over to the side of the road. I sit in my car, in a parking lot, crying. I am not able to think about anything, just the tears running down my face. I think it was fifteen or twenty minutes later, I pull myself together and drive to the spa. I go inside, and my girls (employees) are there. They immediately ask, "Carla, what is wrong?"

I cannot talk and say, "I just need to go to my office for a bit, I will explain later." I call my mother to let her know I am all right. She tells me that this is a special day as Andre, my dead brother, was born on December 21 and he would have been 50 this year. I have this inner knowing, this knowledge that it was my brother, Andre, reaching out to me on this clear, cold winter's day to say that he is with me, that I am not alone. For seeing a rainbow on a winter's day when there is no rain and the skies are clear is unheard of. Yes, the universe is reaching out to me. I am blessed. It was within a couple of weeks of this happening that Nyceim moved in with me to continue our spiritual journey together.

Nyceim, I have to say, really assisted me into diving deep into spirituality. He was a wealth of information. We would sit on the bed with a plate of crackers, cheese and vegetables and go down the rabbit hole with YouTube videos. Watching a video would consist of listening to it for a few minutes and then discussing what was said for about ten minutes. It got my mind working. It solidified things I had intuitively known. It opened my eyes to the spiritual world around me. We watched videos on Dr. Lew Hen on Ho'oponopono...I am sorry, Please forgive me, Thank you, I love you. This was amazing, and I started doing this on a regular basis.

Nyceim introduced me to the theory behind the number 11:11 as I had been seeing it for a while. In simple terms, 11:11 is an awakening code. Those who see this code are driven to research it and if they research it they will see that it is intended to awaken the human species to the new energies that are evolving in the world. This resonated with me and anyone who knows me has had conversations on 11:11 with me. We watched David Icke, The Secret, Abraham Hicks, conspiracy theories, and much, much more. Nyceim was my awakening code. I truly believe that the universe brought him into my existence to supply me with knowledge and open myself up. It also taught me lessons on how much I still had to release and let go as Nyceim also triggered my old belief systems, which released a seething pot of negative emotions out. I projected them onto him. While some of the reasons may have been valid, the way in which I dealt with them was not as I had not fully dealt with the layers of trauma from my past. When these layers are triggered, they can become like a volcano, erupting all the old hurts and pain and projecting them out to hurt the one that is hurting you. I am not proud of these reactions but I can look back and see why and how they happened, and the ability to see from a clearer perspective allows one to focus on releasing them. It is this understanding that allows me to move forward.

Nyceim and I eventually parted ways. He left to go and find himself. He packed up his suburban with his dog and what little belongings he had, and started traveling west. He had no idea where he was going. He had started his journey and was about an hour or so outside of St. Albert; I drove out there and we spent a wonderful last day and night together in the back of his suburban. We lost touch for a while. But a soul partner is never gone for long. We still keep in touch and have wonderfully long, in-depth spiritual conversations.

Wayne—Wayne and I met through Rene. I was at a spiritual trade show one weekend and Rene was there with his energy boards and doing energetic readings with one of his machines. He was sharing a booth with Wayne. Wayne was there with his energy tools. There was a huge lineup of people waiting to see Wayne. I was intrigued, so I stood in line. I have a great logical mind, so I typically approach new things with a bit of skepticism. Wayne has these energy rings and when you stand on one ring and place the other ring over your head you can feel a shift of energy. All the while he is telling you what is going on and why and how it is affecting you. I have not felt anything like this before. I talk to him and he gives me his card.

A couple of months later, I call him up and he meets me at the spa. He brings some of his energy tools with him. We have an extremely long conversation about the tools and what Wayne does. He is out there, one has to really think or, I should say, one has to go with their inner intuition and energy in order to perceive where Wayne is coming from. It feels right, but I would have no way of explaining what it is he actually does. I buy a few of his tools and start utilizing them. During this conversation he tells me that I was placed here, on this planet, to assist in the evolution of the energies. I am to play a large role in healing the world. Even though he did not say I am a healer, the feelings are still there. Guess what my mind says.

A few months go by, maybe six or more. Wayne comes walking into my spa saying that he has been thinking of me and he is there because he has been told he needs to see me. We sit in my office and continue to have a very long conversation. You see, conversations with Wayne are never short. They are always at least an hour or two in duration and it feels like you are floating in the etheric realm.

This relationship of ours continues like this. One day I will feel the need to talk to him and then I will call. The next time it would be him doing the calling. I have been blessed enough to have been asked to visit his house. He lives out in the country with his partner. Their entire place is full of energy, it is a magical place and I love visiting and seeing him.

Lynn – It is fall of 2010, I am at home and devastated. Things are not going well at the spa. Money is always an issue. I am tired, and I am upset, and I feel that I have been going backwards. I understand that my poor little nine-year-old child has been turning up in my life with pain. I have a lot of pain. I am tired of freaking out. I yell at the universe to give me some kind of help in releasing the old pain, to let me live the life I am meant to live without the old stuff coming back at me. I have a conversation with Rene and I ask him if he knows of anyone who assists in releasing old beliefs. He does, he recommends Lynn who lives in Playa del Carmen, MX. He calls her and then calls me back to set up an appointment with her. I do this right away and I have an appointment the next day. What she did seemed to help and, as it turned out, she was traveling to Edmonton within the next two weeks to hold a weekend workshop. I go and attend the workshop. She becomes a friend and we hang out every time she comes back to Edmonton. Lynn led a major role in me moving to Playa del Carmen.

Deepak—I think it was April or May of 2011. I was working at the front desk in my spa. It was early afternoon and the spa was slow. It was warm and sunny outside. This man walks in. He is Indian and holding a business card that said tarot readings, palm readings, and a couple of other things. I looked at it and, before he said anything, I said, "No, thank you, I am not interested." He then starts talking and telling me things about myself, things that no one else knew about and that I have never uttered a word about. So I asked how much. He said that I could pay whatever I thought it was worth. He has an ashram in India and he helps orphaned and abandoned children. He travels through different countries raising money by offering readings.

I gave in and invited him into my office. His name was Deepak. He was with me for at least three hours telling me all sorts of things about me, the present, the past and the future. At one point he tore the corner off a piece of paper and wrote some things on it and crunched it into a ball and put it on the corner of my desk. At this time, Nyceim was staying with me. Deepak asked me questions about myself as well as the same questions for Nyceim. The questions were on the lines of favorite color, favorite number, etc. However, his last question was directed at me. What did I most want for myself? After I answered the questions he took the ball of paper and put it in my hand and had me blow on it three times. After this, I was to open it. On the piece of paper were my answers to all of the questions he had asked, including my answer to his last question. This answer was, "To not have my past beliefs and hurts affect my present anymore."

I was astounded. While I do not remember much more of what we talked about, there are a couple of other significant things he said that have submerged themselves into my memory. First, he said that I would be getting a new car in a couple of months. I immediately thought, *OK well, now I do not believe. I have never owned a new car in my life, there is no need.* Also, my car was running just fine. Why would I get rid of it? Lastly, I was a business owner with no salary, no one would give me a loan. Yes, some doubt crept in. A couple of months later, I was driving on the highway and the engine of my car blew up. I got it towed to a garage and had someone look at it. Yup, engine was gone and would cost a lot of money to fix, more than the car was worth. I am devastated. I need to get to work every day. I need a car. I talk to one of my staff and they know someone at a car dealership and suggested I call. I did. They took my information, then did a credit check. Came back to say that I was approved and there were three or four different cars that I could get financing for. This is how I got a brand new car—approximately two months after Deepak told me I would. I am now back to a being a believer again.

The other thing I remember clearly is that he told me I was a healer. *OMG, not this again,* I thought. I told him I did not think that it was true and the reasons why. That didn't bother him. He also said that I built Divine Body Spa as a place of healing. I was attracting all kinds of souls, some of them spiritual souls that had a purpose in my life and this was the way that enabled them to contact me. This I now know is true as the amount of people who I have been blessed to meet through Divine Body Spa and to continue to have in my life is simply amazing.

When Deepak left, we exchanged phone numbers and email addresses. I was a little in shock and awe after he left. I told Nyceim about him that night. I also told my beautiful soul sister Jacinta. Jacinta was intrigued and made me realize that it was not coincidence that he had come into my spa. She wanted to know if I could contact him as she would like to get a reading from him. I called the next day and he answered. He was in England. He left the country right after he saw me. What are the odds that an Indian who has an ashram in India knocks on the door of a spa that is in a strip mall in Edmonton, AB? Makes one think.

It has now been just over six years since that reading. Over those six years I have received phone calls and emails from him checking in to see how I am doing.

There are many other people who randomly came up and told me I am a healer during my time at the spa, so much so that I got confused and angry.

CHAPTER 32

January and July 2011

New Vision and Week of Gifting

I was doing some Google searches on the number 11:11. I come across a site that will be doing monthly online meditations on the eleventh day of each month at 11:11 am. This intrigues me and I sign up to attend as it is free. January 11, 2011 comes about and I go into one of the massage rooms, lie down on the bed, put my headphones on and get ready for the meditation. The actual call starts earlier as there is a preamble on the significance of 11:11 and what these meditations will do for people. The actual guided meditation starts at 11:11. We are guided to a deep level of relaxation and then they tell us to picture ourselves in the future. It could be a month, six months, a year, two years, it does not matter, allow ourselves to go into the future. Do not just see yourself there; you have to be there, in the future, to feel it, to smell it, to sense it, to hear it as if you are actually there. I find myself outside a house on the grass, I can smell the grass. I am doing yoga and beside me are palm trees waving in the wind. I can smell the sea breeze washing gently over me as I am doing my yoga moves. I know that the ocean is just beyond the trees. I have a feeling of bliss, of calm, of contentedness. I keep that visualization with me for the next year or so until it manifested, just like my visualization of my perfect house with the perfect kids manifested.

The last couple of weeks at the spa had been stressful. Not having a car and the business not doing great. I am not sure why, but the universe sent me many messages this week. All the messages coming were on the lines of, "We see you, we feel you, we love you." Well, at least that was the impression I got. On July 21 I got my new car. On July 22 Dan sent me a huge bouquet of flowers to congratulate me on the car. On July 22 Jacinta gave me a beautiful bracelet. On July 23 a friend of mine had just gone salmon fishing and brought me a huge piece of salmon. On July 23 Dan gave me a silver bracelet that used to belong to his mom. July 24, I found a ring that I had lost about a year ago. It was tucked inside the seam of my chair. July 25, I found the wooden pendant that Deepak had given me, I had made it into a bracelet and it had fallen off my arm a week before. It is things like this that make me marvel at the strangeness of it all. Synchronicity? Coincidence? Message from the universe? Who is to know?

CHAPTER 33

September 2011

The End of Divine Body Spa

September 2011, I am tired, exhausted in fact. I had been working 24/7 for two and a half years straight. I had tried hiring managers to take some stress off of me, but they had not worked out. I knew deep down that I could not do it anymore. I had also run out of money. In fact, I had spent the majority of my savings as well as most of the equity in my house to keep the spa running. I was at my wits' end. I decided that I needed to let it go. One option was to just walk away, close the doors and just leave. However, the universe had another plan for me. Someone was willing to buy the spa. We had meetings; they said that they would do the best for me. Instead, at the last minute, they tried low-balling me. I decided that I would prefer to just close the doors than sell to them as their true colors were shown. At the last moment, a friend of mine, who owned a business in the next strip mall, made me an offer. She was honest and trustworthy, and we came to an agreement.

On the day that I was signing the papers, I received a call from the chairman of the board of Serenic. You see, he had been calling me every six months since I left to see if I wanted to come back to work for them. This time, however, when he made me the offer, I said that I would pursue it. The only thing holding me back was that I needed to be convinced that the environment had changed, that the reasons for me leaving in the first place had been looked after. Serenic bought me a ticket to Denver, where the head office was, and I interviewed the president and vice president of sales for Serenic in the airport. I went home; they made me an offer and I took it. Thank you, universe. At this time, I was still in debt. I had about $15,000 in credit card debt, I owed my brother $5,000 that he lent me, and I really had no savings or equity left in my house. I had lost everything. This was actually a blessing. As I looked back at all my scrimping and saving and not doing things because "I have no money", I decided at that point that I would not let money have the influence it used to have on me. As I was down to nothing I released the energy of needing to have money, of needing to have savings, of not being able to do anything. When I did that, some miraculous things happened to me. I started receiving money from sources that no one would have ever thought of—enough money, over three years, to be able to quit my job and travel the world for a year. Do I believe that there is an energy, a power, greater than me? Yes, I do, for I have been given so many, many signs that I would be utterly stupid not to believe.

At the same time as I was selling my business, Dan offered to take me away to Mexico for a couple of weeks. He had seen the toll that the spa had taken on me. I said yes. Before I started working for Serenic I went on an incredible two-week vacation to Cancun and Playa del Carmen.

CHAPTER 34

October to November 2011

First Visit to Playa del Carmen

I was not supposed to be in Mexico on Nov 11. Dan and I should have left Mexico and returned to Canada before then. The universe conspired to delay our flight to Mexico by having a hurricane warning on the day we were to travel. So we delayed leaving that day and booked another flight. As it turned out, I was blessed to be on the top of a temple in Ek Balam sitting in a doorway meditating on November 11, 2011 at 11:11:11:11...

I went up to sit in the doorway at about 11:00am and started my meditation. A tour group had just arrived, and I could hear them coming up the temple; Dan was below talking to the tour leader, telling him that I had come all the way from Canada to do this meditation at this exact date and time and asked if he could clear the group from the temple. He did. As I sat there meditating, I felt a surge of energy going throughout my whole being. At that moment, it started to rain. A light rain. I could feel the earth cleansing and I was united with all of those who were also meditating at that time. It was an amazing feeling. I stopped meditating at about 11:20. I was floating. The power of what had just happened has no explanation. For the rest of the day I floated around with this beautiful glowing feeling. This feeling is embedded into my being and I am honored to have been able to be a part of this moment. I felt as one with everything. I AM...truly blessed and awed.

When in Playa del Carmen, Dan and I were invited to supper at Lynn's house. Lynn is the girl who Rene introduced me to and she assisted me in getting over some of my past beliefs. She found out that I worked from home. For six months after we had returned to Canada Lynn kept sending me condo rentals in Playa saying that I should move down. The first few she sent me I was thinking, *Yeah, move to Mexico, ha that will never happen.*

One day, in July 2012, she called me and told me she'd just met someone who was renting a condo. She had not yet given the rental to a property management company. She was going to do this in a couple of days if she did not find someone herself. I started conversing with her, got the pictures, and it seemed too good to be true. I figured I had nothing to lose. On Monday, in the afternoon, I called my boss, brought him out of a meeting and told him that I had an offer to move to Mexico and asked if Serenic would allow me to work from there. I told him all the reasons why he should let me go. But I needed to know within the next day. He asked if he could have two days to check some things out; I said, "OK." He came back to me within two days and said yes, Serenic would allow me to work from Mexico. I signed the contract to lease the condo for a year and started making plans to move down for October 2012. I have to say that it was not easy as I had been living in my house with the kids for ten years. I had a lot of things to purge and pack and store. It was a very hectic time of my life.

CHAPTER 35

December 21, 2012

End of the Mayan Calendar

December 21, 2012, the end of the Mayan calendar, the change of energies from the patriarchal to the matriarchal. The twenty-first is on a Friday; the Monday before I felt that there was something special that I needed to do in order to assist in bringing in the new energies. What, I had no idea. I did not want to go and pay to see anything as that did not feel real. I let go of the thought. I believed that if I was to be a part of anything it would happen, without my interference. On Thursday, Dec 20 nothing had come along yet, so I decided that if nothing happened I would go on Saturday to the beach and meditate by myself. I was happy with that thought.

Thursday night, I went for supper with a friend. She was a restaurant/bar owner. During supper she was saying that she was closing down her restaurant for the weekend. She and her cook were going down to Bacalar, three hours south of Playa del Carmen, for some kind of ceremony; they would be camping and staying the weekend. I asked what kind of ceremony, but she did not know. For her, it was just a getaway. I instinctively knew it had to do with the end of the Mayan calendar. I asked if I could go with them. "Of course," she said. They were leaving at around 11:00 the next day.

Friday morning, I got on the phone with my boss and asked for the day off. "Of course," he said. I love the universe! As I was packing to go, I decided to bring along some crystals, gems and stones that I had picked up on my journeys.

We leave a bit later than planned, but that is the Mexican way. We get to the camp site and it is getting dark. We get out of the car and the ceremony has already started. There was a Mayan Shaman and an Aztec Shaman doing a ceremony as well as fifteen or twenty Mayan and Aztec people. An altar was placed beside the lagoon. I asked if I could place my treasures on the altar. "Of course," I was told. I was the only person at the ceremony who only spoke English. There were only a couple of people who spoke a bit of English. The entire ceremony was in Spanish and Mayan. Although I did not understand the words that were being said I did feel the energy and I understood what was happening during the blessings. We spent three days and two nights doing ceremony.

The next day, they were building a temazcal. This is like a sweat lodge but Mexican style. There was a ceremony to bless the wood and the fire and the rocks that went into the temazcal. Some people had brought traditional clothes to wear for the ceremony. The blessing included talking, singing, and dancing. I was taken by the hand to join in. We all were one. The singing and dancing got moved into a large, open, green grass field. The energy was amazing. The ceremonies in the temazcal were held on the second night. I did not partake as I felt it was something that I was not ready for at that time.

CHAPTER 36

October 2012 to 2013

Life in Playa

The actual move to Playa del Carmen was fairly painless. I only knew one person there, Lynn. She had just gotten into a new relationship and was spending all of her time with her new man. This, I understood. I was invited over for supper once and maybe out a couple of times. But soon after I moved I did not see or hear from her unless we ran into each other. Things had changed. I am fine with this as I am used to being alone. Work keeps me busy during the days.

The cost of things in Mexico is really inexpensive; I get a maid to clean the apartment every week. I also get a yoga instructor to come to my house for private yoga lessons two or three times a week. I go for walks along 5th Avenue at nights and sit and have supper alone. I take the leftovers home and have them for lunch the next day. I go to the beach on weekends and I meditate. The first few months are just getting used to the new town. On Fridays, I go to the local bar and have a couple of drinks and dance. I come home by myself.

My yoga instructor, at the time, is Mexican but she speaks really good English so there is no language barrier. One day, she asked me if I wanted to come with her to see a tarot card reader. She raved about this person. I had not had my cards read by anyone for a long time so I agreed. We head down to Cancun and go to this woman's house. I sit down and the first thing she says to me is, "You are a healer."

OMG, not this again, I thought. You see, I work from home with Serenic so I do not get to interact with a lot of people outside of work. I have not heard anyone say this to me in a couple of years, and the confusion and anger around this matter has subsided. Ah well, I am not going to let this affect me. So I just say, "Sure."

I start taking trips down to Tulum. Tulum has a wonderful spiritual energy. The white, sandy beaches go on forever. I go there and read, take long walks, go in the ocean, meditate. It is peaceful and calm. I tried to go at least once a month and stay for one night. Tulum is the place where I realized that my second vision had come true. Me practicing yoga beside the ocean. The universe works in mysterious ways. Tulum is also the place where I realized how much I had changed since I moved to Mexico. I had become one with myself. I actually liked my own company. While I was alone a lot, I no longer felt lonely. I did not have that neediness inside me anymore to be with anyone. I was at peace.

I date someone for a while, he is from Germany. He lives in Playa during the winter and goes back to Germany in the summer. I date him anyway. It only lasts a couple of months. We break up when he leaves to go back to Germany the next summer.

Soon after, I run into another man, Sharky, he is twenty years older than me. Sharky has been around Playa del Carmen for about twenty years and is well-known to the local expat crowd. He has led a fast and vivid life. He is very intelligent, funny, extremely personable and he has an interest in me. In the beginning, we had run into each other a couple of times and had some minor conversations. One night, I had gone to a singing bowl meditation with a friend.

We then went over to one of the local bars. The loud music and ambiance was not resonating with me so I was planning on leaving. Sharky is there and we start having a conversation. Then he asks me if I want to go over to his place, he has a rooftop where we could sit and talk in quiet. I was a little hesitant, but I did end up going. We sat there and talked for an hour or so, and then I went home. We went out a few times and then started dating on a regular basis.

There is one major item that happened earlier on in the relationship that made me fall madly in love with Sharky. I had not had a serious relationship for a long time and I had done enough work on myself to know the areas I need to improve on when I am in a relationship. One main item is the ability to speak my truth when a situation arises and I get triggered. I need to learn how to talk, how to let my voice be heard, to be understood. I was bound and determined to put this into practice. After all of these years I was not going to push my feelings down anymore. Something happened, I am not sure what it was, but I was triggered and felt hurt. I sat down with Sharky and told him how much I appreciated him. I created a warm, loving environment. Then I told him that I had a hard time getting my feelings out into words, that this may take some time and I may go silent for a while. I asked him to be patient while I found the right words to say. He agreed and I started. I told him that something had happened which made me feel hurt, be it right or be it wrong, I was hurt. I was not blaming him, or pointing fingers at him or being angry at him, but I wanted him to know what happened in order to make me feel this way. I also told him that I would never say anything to hurt him intentionally and he needed to remember that, for if I were to say anything that triggered him it would not be done with intention and I was there to talk it through with him.

Now it is time for me to tell my feelings, to let my voice be heard. It is hard, I can feel my throat tightening. I know I need to say the right words, in the right way, so as not to have any type of blame pointed at Sharky. I have gone through enough counseling to know that one should never say the "you" word, as in, "You did this" and, "You did that." For as soon as one starts a sentence with, "You did…" the other person automatically becomes defensive and stops listening. I start slowly, the first couple of words come out, and then I pause for a long time, trying to make sense of the jumble of feelings inside myself in order to put words to them. I say another couple of words, I start and stop a few times. Sharky is sitting there, patiently, watching, not saying anything and not pushing for more. This gives me the strength to start talking more fluidly and then the words get attached to the emotions and it all comes flooding out. At the end, I say, "I needed to let you know how I was feeling so that you understand why I got upset. Be it right or be it wrong, you now have an understanding of where that came from."

This is the first time in my life that I have been able to talk about a present day hurt in order to release the energy, rather than pushing it down and storing the negative energy for a blowout later. Sharky gave the best response ever, he said that he now understood and he would make it a point not to do or say whatever it was that triggered me in the first place. At this moment, I felt lighter, I felt free, I felt like a huge weight had been lifted from my shoulders. What once would have been a brick in the wall to come out under anger had now dissipated in the light and love that surrounded us. This is the gift that Sharky gave me. This is the reason I fell madly in love with him.

Unfortunately, this was the only time we reached this space. Any attempts made to get back to this place were thwarted. I kept hoping and I kept trying but I could not make it happen again, and so the relationship ended. We still remain friends, although it has been hard sometimes as Playa del Carmen is a small town and the expat community even smaller. The feeling of being able to talk and open up freely and let my voice be heard has given me hope, hope that I can talk, I can let my voice be heard and understood. For it is the understanding of why something happened, what that person was going through in order for it to happen, which allows the hurt and the pain to be released.

CHAPTER 37

2014 to October 2015

Selling my House and Work

When I left St. Albert, I had hired a property management company to look after my house. They had now been looking after my house for two years, and I was constantly fighting with them for the excessive charges for fixing things in the house. In the spring of 2014, I needed to get some work done in the basement. I would not let the property management company contract it out, so I found a company to do the work and I asked Dan if he would mind going over to supervise. I had heard from someone that the housing market in St. Albert was good for sellers. I asked Dan if he knew of any real estate agents and if so maybe he could get someone to come in and determine if I could get a good price for it. The house got put on the market and it sold within a week. It is things like this that make me think of the universe and it guiding me in directions that I would not normally go. I was being released and set free of material burden. This came more into a bigger understanding in the next year, as you will see.

It is 2014, and work is going exceptionally well. I am meeting all of my quotas and getting a bonus every month. My savings are starting to show some form of growth. I am happy in what I am doing. I am good at what I do. I work with Microsoft partners in Canada, the USA, Ethiopia, Guatemala, Lebanon, and El Salvador. I recruit new partners to sell the payroll and HR software that we develop. I assist them in selling the software. I train them in how to sell. I demonstrate the software for larger deals. I am at the top of my game; my partners are wonderful and I have a great deal of respect for them. I am not micro managed and the feeling of independence is wonderful. I finish off the year meeting all of my quotas and getting another nice bonus. I am happy.

In the fall of 2014, our company gets acquired by a Canadian owned firm. It shocked and surprised me that the company who acquired us was Bellamy, the company I had worked at for a short time just after I finished my computer systems technology degree. As with any acquisition, there were staff changes and procedural changes. Some of these changes upset my partners, and it was not an easy transition as a lot of my time was now spent working with disgruntled partners. Obviously, the sales went down, this was to be expected. In spring 2015, I thought I would be let go and I was fine with this idea. I flippantly thought that I would take some time off and go travel the world. I have never thought of doing this before and I honestly have no idea where this thought came from.

Later that year, I was talking with my boss and he said that they were happy with the sales that were coming through, I was doing a good job and to keep it up. I, on the other hand, was becoming increasingly unhappy with the situation. I took that flippant thought of traveling the world and started making it a reality. At nights and on the weekends, I would research places to go and different things that I would like to see. I created a spreadsheet and started putting down all of the low, high and shoulder seasons and any other pertinent information about each place. I printed off a map and highlighted all of the places I was thinking of. I then

Googled the places that I had no idea where in the world they were and highlighted them on the map. I researched, and I planned, and I got excited. This was going to happen.

In July 2015, I called my boss and told him that I was going to take a year off work and travel the world. I quit my job. The ability of selling my house the year before and getting rid of material possessions was also a huge factor that allowed the thought of traveling the world to become a reality.

CHAPTER 38

October 2015 to September 2016

Travel the World

I am pretty logical and analytical when it comes to planning. I had multiple spreadsheets and have researched lots of travel sights. There are so many things one needs to know when traveling the world. I contact a travel agent that specializes in around-the-world travel. He helped me set out my itinerary. I decide to buy all the airline tickets that I need to travel for the first three months. I need to have that little bit of planning to make me feel more confident as I travel. I decide that after this amount of time I could buy my transportation on the fly as I knew which countries I wanted to go to after that.

All of I sudden, I decide that I need to get my scuba diving license as I would be traveling to some of the best dive areas in the world. It would be a waste to miss that part. Me, who three years ago would not enter any type of water that would be above my head without going into a panic attack. Me, the person who needed her hand held while wearing a life vest for snorkeling. Now I am going to scuba dive. Never say never. I finished my open water certification about two weeks before leaving and I went on my first two dives after certification in Cozumel. I find out that I love the underwater world. I ended up having thirty-six dives all over the world, in some of the best diving sites, as well as getting my advanced open water certification in Koh Tao, Thailand.

I give the lease of my condo to a friend and put my stuff in storage. On October 17, 2015, I hop on a plane in Cancun with my suitcase and backpack, and all of my belongings that are supposed to last me a year, and I head off to my first destination, which is San Jose, Costa Rica.

Here is my itinerary from October 17, 2015 to January 17, 2016:

Five cities in Costa Rica, three cities in Panama, three cities in Ecuador, including the Galapagos Islands, seven cities in Peru, one city in the Cook Islands, two cities in New Zealand, nine cities in Australia and then Bali. That is eight countries and thirty-one cities in three months. The entire first part of my travel was geared around being in Australia for Christmas. I have relatives there on my mother's side, aunts and uncles whom I had maybe met once or twice, and cousins that I had never met.

First stop in Australia is Melbourne to see my aunt, uncle and two cousins. I stayed with one of my cousins and his significant other. They were awesome hosts and I got along extremely well with him. We stayed up late at night talking, I heard so many stories about my mother and my father and relatives that I had never heard of before. They all confirmed what I had learned about Uncle Rex and his penchant for little girls. However, it did not just stop at little girls, as I was told, there were many other women old and young that he aspired to. I am so glad I did all the work on myself regarding this person as it could have thrown me into an abyss.

I also found out that two of my cousins, both male, and I were all born within one month of each other in the same year. Why did I never know this? Doesn't matter really. After Melbourne, I go to Sydney and Byron Bay, then off to the Gold Coast to visit with my aunt and more cousins. My aunt had more stories about my mother that I did not know. The pieces started to fall into place, the understanding of why or how became clearer. With that understanding comes a sense of peace and letting go. The ability of changing perspective about my mother and what had happened.

By the time I got to Bali I was exhausted, mentally and physically. I decided to do a month-long ayurvedic cleanse and retreat. There I was able to reset my body and my mind as being in one place for that long was heavenly. The tourist visa for Bali is only for thirty days. I had been at the retreat for thirty days and had not seen much more of Bali, so I decided to leave the country and come back to do some more touristy things. I head off to Singapore, the place that I always knew I would visit but was hesitant to commit to when planning my trip.

What to say about Singapore? It is large and expensive and clean. I stayed in my first pod hostel. A tiny cubicle to lie in. It is a good thing I am not claustrophobic. I loved Singapore Zoo. I got to feed a giraffe, yes, I love animals. Three days and two nights was enough. I did not have any a-ha moments or feelings of familiarity. I was just a baby when I was last there and it had changed drastically in fifty years. My knowing that I would go back some day was now made into reality.

I went back to Bali and continued my journey. Gili Islands, Northern Thailand, Laos, Vietnam, Cambodia, Southern Thailand, seven countries up the east coast of Africa doing Safari, Hungary, Croatia, Albania, Montenegro, Greece, Turkey, Netherlands and then back to Canada and finally home to Playa del Carmen late September 2016. I made a journal entry for every day of my trip; each entry has the date, the country, the city, the hostel I stayed in and what happened on that day. I took pictures, thousands of pictures. I posted pictures to Facebook whenever I had good

Internet. I captured enough stories and memories to write another book. It was a trip of a lifetime, one that most people only dream of. While it had never been a dream of mine I am truly blessed to have had the chance, truly blessed to be open enough to allow, to follow the path that had been laid before me, to say yes and jump.

CHAPTER 39

October 2016 to November 2017

Playa del Carmen

2017 has been a hard year on me. Everything that I tried, I failed at. Well, at least that was my thought pattern until I realized that the universe was not going to allow me to find things that would distract me from writing this book.

I got back to Playa from my around-the-world trip in late September 2016. I rented a friend's place for October and then I found a small one-bedroom apartment that I stayed at for six months. I took the first two months off from finding work so that I could get some rest. The travel took a lot out of me. Then I decided I would take December off as well. Now comes January 2017, I still have no idea what I want to do for work. I know that I cannot go back to the type of work I was doing. I was not willing to go back into the rat race just for the sake of making money. I had changed. Something had shifted inside of me. But there was nothing calling to me. Nothing saying, "Hey, this is what you need to do." I wanted to do something that I was passionate about, where I could wake up every day with a smile on my face and enjoy what I was doing. I had no idea what it was that would do this for me.

I decided to hire a career coach, and for two months he had

me writing about my passions, my dreams, where I saw myself in the future. I came to the realization that I wanted to help. People, the planet, the environment, whatever. I would be most passionate if I could give back. The trouble came from not knowing what types of jobs were available based on my wants and needs. I had already decided that I would not move back to Canada. I would stay in Playa del Carmen. I went on every site that I could find that offered remote work. Lo and behold, the majority of work was what I was doing before. I started to panic a little and started sending my resume to any job that I thought I was qualified for. I never got one response. At that time, I realized that my resume was not even getting looked at as I did not have the education. *Hmm, I have been here before.* Most employers were looking for some type of university degree. I have a two-year college diploma. It doesn't matter that I had experience, because my resume never made the first cut. I worked long and hard on updating my resume and spent hours creating job specific cover letters. I researched how I could contact HR departments or hiring managers so that I could put a personal touch to it. Nothing worked. After a couple of months of working on this consistently I became discouraged.

Soon after, I came across a girl in Playa who was working a multi-level marketing (MLM) job that had to do with saving the planet by having people purchase solar power for their house. *Great,* I thought, *I love the idea.* The job was to get people who own their own homes to have an estimate done on their house for installing solar panels. The company was currently only in certain states in the US; however, they were adding states all the time and then would be moving into Canada and Australia. Wow, this was meant to be as I have lots of contacts in the US, I lived in Canada for years, and I have relatives in Australia. I bought a new laptop, set up a Skype number, updated my Linked In account and started creating a spreadsheet of all the contacts that I could talk to. I learned all I could about solar power and started creating emails that I could send to my contacts. Unfortunately, a lot of my contacts were not in the states where the company was already set up. I also ran into a lot of road blocks. All the people that got excited had to wait for that state to open up. Once again discouragement set in.

I had to leave Mexico in March 2017 as my tourist visa was expiring. I decided that I would get my temporary residency visa for Mexico. You need to apply for this from your home country. I went back to Canada to do this. While in Edmonton I visited a few friends. I had another idea that started percolating in my brain. I would set up retreats in Mexico. One of the friends I visited with was the person who purchased Divine Body Spa from me. We had a wonderful conversation and I was talking about the idea of retreats with her. She was excited about the idea and suggested that I talk to Susan. Susan used to be a representative for one of the skin care lines that I carried in the spa. When she came to the spa on her normal rounds, we would have long conversations about spirituality in my office. I loved those visits.

I contacted Susan and she loved the idea of retreats. She and her husband had just set up their own business and had been talking about doing something like this. She also said that they had a vision of setting up a website that would offer all kinds of courses on spirituality, from beginner to master. She said that they had lots of content for the website but did not have the technical knowledge to set it up. Susan had seen me in action with the spa as I handled my own website and all of my own marketing. She had faith that I could get the job done. I had not been doing any type of marketing or work on websites since Divine Body Spa. I was not as confident as she was. Susan and her husband were going on a road trip soon, so I suggested they let me do some research and we would talk when they got back. I spent that month researching all the different methods of marketing. I took Facebook Blueprint courses; I researched webinar software; I researched e-course software. I gained confidence that I could make this work. When they got back, I gave Susan a summary of what I found out and what I had done. Rather than paying me for the work she suggested that I become a partner. I would get one-third of the profits from the business. A deal was done and away I went. I created the website and the Facebook page; I created spiritual posts that would go on the Facebook page, one for every day. I worked my ass off. However, content never came. They were having a hard time making the content interesting. I made suggestions, we had Skype calls and phone calls. Still nothing came. I knew they were at a standstill. I was at a standstill as well for I could not do anything more without content. I decided that I should make a trip up to see them to help figure things out. After our visit, I thought that they would be fine to move things along. Content never did come. Once again, I am at a place of discouragement.

During that trip to see Susan I also got to visit my beautiful Sherry. We had a wonderful visit and she gave me a reading—the reading that made me realize I needed to start my book, the book that I was told to write years ago in one of my first readings from her; the book that came up every time I had a reading from her. It was time, no more procrastination. It was then that I discovered the universe was not going to let me off easy. The reason for all the failed attempts was to get me focused on writing. It would not allow anything to get in my way, which also included men—for any relationship, all of two, that I entered into ended quickly. It was soon after the reading with Sherry that I started writing.

The reading was recorded and here are a couple of excerpts from the beginning of it:

"Didn't it come before, about you writing a book?" Sherry channels.

"Yes" I state. I sit in awe that this is coming about again.

"This is about you, your journey. The journey of a soul. The journey of your soul. It needs to be told because you have got the recipe for how to overcome and how to become."

I sit quietly in amazement as I am listening to this.

Sherry continues "Don't let the word 'book' scare you into not doing this. They are saying memoir. This memoir of the spirit that you are and the journey that you have been on since earth. Since as early as you can remember and all of those pivotal moments and all the challenges and how you made it through them."

The reading goes on for another hour. But the message has been clear, the book, my memoir, needs to be written and the time is NOW.

CHAPTER 40

December 2017

My Playa Family and Soul Sisters

Playa del Carmen has a large expat community, people from all over the world who have decided to move to paradise. It is the most multicultural place that I have ever lived in. There is a variety of people from all sorts of backgrounds living here. It is multidimensional. One of the things that we all have in common is that we are all away from our home countries, from our families. This, I believe, is why we have become one big family within this community. We hang out at the same bars, we have parties at one another's houses, we go on road trips together, and we care about each other.

It is this family environment, along with the spiritual energy that surrounds this place that has made me decide to live here, to make Playa my home.

I have to stress the importance of having people in your life with whom you can be you. To let down your hair, take off your mask and be vulnerable with. For most of my life I paid people to listen to me, to see me without my mask, to allow my voice to be heard. My Playa soul sisters need a special mention for they have listened to me, allowed me to shed my tears, laughed with me, understood me and never once judged me.

Antonella, has been living in Playa for over twenty years. She was recommended to me for yoga and massage the second year that I was in Playa. She would come over two to three times a week for private yoga lessons, and then once a week for massage. It was Antonella's yoga and massage that fixed a rotator cuff injury that had been bothering me for fifteen years. Our friendship grew from a business to a personal level. Even when we stopped the yoga she would come over and spend time on the couch with me, talking. My couch became a place of comfort, of openness where we could tell each other exactly what we were going through and offer a loving space for letting out what was within, and assistance or advice on any issues. One of my original Playa soul sisters, although our communication has become sporadic, she will always have a space in my heart.

Janelle, aka Nellie, and I met at Mom's bar around fall 2013. She was from Canada and was leaving to go back the next day. We hit it off immediately. She got back in touch with me during her next trip to Playa and we hung out and got to know each other more. Our relationship grew into a beautiful bond as we are both spiritual and have been through a lot, sitting on her patio with drinks in hand, crying and releasing, being open and honest. There is something to be said about having that safe space with a non-judgmental person in order to let your feelings out. It creates a bond that is beyond words.

Francis, beautiful Francis, does not live in Playa del Carmen, she lives in Lierop, Netherlands. However, she has been to Playa about four times now on vacation over the last three years. The first time I met her I immediately felt comfortable. Each time she came back to Playa we would get together. We started chatting on Facebook and having drinks through Skype when she was back in the

Netherlands. Our relationship grew each and every time we spoke. My last stop on my around-the-world trip was the Netherlands. I stayed with Francis for a week at her place relaxing and talking, all the while our bond growing rapidly. The distance does not matter as we have been there for each other multiple times. The Internet, Facebook, Whatsapp, and Skype bring the world closer together. I am truly blessed to have met her and have her in my life.

This poem was inspired by a conversation with my beautiful soul sister Francis while I was writing the book. I dedicate it to her…

Ship without Sails

A ship without sails
abreast in the breeze,
not knowing where it is going,
flowing with ease.

This is how life should be,
no intent and no course
to flow with the currents
to get where you need.

To remove the mind
and listen to the heart
this is where you will find
the bliss that is yours.

Neus moved to Playa permanently a year or so after I did, albeit she had been coming to Playa for many years. Being from Valencia, Spain, Spanish is her first language and her English was limited and so when we first met our conversations were sparse. I always liked her as she was this spark of energy, always happy and smiling and making you feel good just with her presence. When I got back from my around-the-world trip, her English had greatly improved and we got to know each other on a more personal level. Neus is one of the most generous, kindhearted people I know. She will be there for you in a heartbeat if you need her. Even if you don't reach out she will know that there is something wrong and then just come knocking on your door with food, or drink, and always a smile. I love this girl and she is a major part of my soul sister tribe.

Susan has been living in Playa del Carmen for about twenty years. She is this beautiful, intelligent, vibrant being. We knew of each other for a long time, however, never really talked until 2017. It was during a wonderful conversation on her balcony that we realized how connected we actually were. We were talking about how it does not matter where one lives, depression can always arise at any moment and time. What you decide to do with the depression is what makes the difference. Since that conversation she has become a true soul sister, friend and confident. The following is a poem that came forth the day after our initial conversation. I need to preface this poem by stating that during the month of August there were two Tropical Depressions that formed into Tropical Storms within the area that I live.

This poem was inspired by Susan and all my girlfriends who have been through a "tropical depression".

Tropical Depression

A storm is here
deep in my soul,
alone and lonely,
nowhere to go.

I allow it to take over,
lightning flashes in my heart,
storm waves are pounding,
the rain falls from my eyes.

My mind is in turmoil.
Why am I here?
Lost in paradise
in a wall of fear.

I am unable to move,
in a ball I hide,
wrapped in my sorrow
for days I have cried.

What is this feeling
enveloping me?
It is so hard to keep going
unable to be free.

I look over the ocean
in a tropical paradise
feeling sad and lonely,
no end in sight.

A glimmer of strength
from deep down inside
awakes and overtakes
the depression inside.

Look all around you,
look where you live,

acknowledge your friends
with so much to give.

This loneliness you feel
comes from your past,
it is time to feel fully,
you can let your tears flow.

Flow like a river
from deep in your soul
washing away
the sad, lonely you.

A space opens wide
inside your being
to replace all the sadness
with a warm, glowing feeling.

The storm is now over,
you are awash in love,
the love that you give you
makes your heart sigh.

Allow and release,
this is the way to go
to become who you truly are,
your authentic soul.

SUMMARY

It is December 16, 2017 and I am sitting in my writing space, my couch, just inside the patio doors that look out onto palm trees and greenery. The rain is coming down in a torrential downpour outside. It is cleansing. I cannot think of a more fitting time to put the last of my words onto paper. This book, my memoirs, will head off to the proofreader tomorrow. All of the years of ignoring the universe, ignoring the messages, not believing that I can do it, thinking that I am not worthy, it will be done as soon as I finish this summary.

I have told people that I am doing this, writing this book, telling my story, opening up to the world and being vulnerable. I get looks of shock. "Why would you want to do this?" they say. "Why not make it into fiction?" "Why not publish under another name?" Many "why" questions are asked. I listen to them all, the responses resonate from my inner being, from my intuition, my inner knowing. This is my story, people need to hear truth from a true being, to know they are not alone. For this is also their story, not in whole, but in parts, in the emotional parts, in the parts that are hidden, in the parts that they are ashamed to acknowledge. It is these parts that haunt them. That come out of the darkness to unsettle their daily lives. The only way to free these parts, these memories, these beliefs is to give them light and allow them to dissipate.

Allowing others to hear my truth, my understanding of my life, my trials, my tribulations, my strengths, and my weaknesses shows that they are not alone. They are not the only ones. Even if only one person gains some insight, some understanding, my job has been accomplished.

I stand here before you, before all of you, vulnerable and naked in my truth. I have opened myself up; I have let all of the demons out of my closet. I have taken off my mask. This is me. I am not a healer, I am not a writer, I am not a victim. I do not need to put a name to myself as such, as I am much more. I am a multitude of emotions and feelings. I am my past, I am my present. I am the tears falling from the sky as rain, I am the laughter showing up as the stars in the sky, I am the love of the warm breeze as it comes off the ocean. I am you.

I love you
all of you
as I am you
as you are me.

ABOUT THE AUTHOR

Carla Feagan was born in Changi, Singapore on a British RAF Base. After Singapore, her family moved to England and then to Canada when she was seven. Carla has lived all over Western and Central Canada including the North West Territories. She holds an honors degree in Computer Systems Technology and has worked as a salesperson, an accountant, a computer programmer, a manager, and a business owner. In 2015, she left her job to experience her own EAT, PRAY, LOVE journey to twenty-one countries for a year. Carla currently lives and works remotely from Playa del Carmen, MX, understanding the true value in creating the life you want.

Check out Carla's website for resources on healing, pictures related to this memoir and updates on what has happened since her memoirs were written.
http://carlafeagan.com/

If you enjoyed this book, please leave a brief review at your online bookseller of choice. Thanks.

CPSIA information can be obtained
at www.ICGtesting.com
Printed in the USA
FFOW03n2258080418
46204572-47492FF

9 781775 260912